NINE PORTRAITS OF JESUS

Peter Hannan SJ

Nine Portraits of Jesus

NEW REVISED EDITION

the columba press

This new revised edition first published in 2009 by
the columba press
55A Spruce Avenue, Stillorgan Industrial Park,
Blackrock, Co Dublin

Cover by Bill Bolger
Origination by The Columba Press
Printed in Ireland by ColourBooks Ltd, Dublin

ISBN 978 1 85607 649 4

Table of Contents

PART I

PART II

Acknowledgments

I would like to thank all those who directly or indirectly have helped me to paint these nine portraits of Jesus. I think particularly of the influence of my parents, of the inspiration and encouragement of my family, of the vision of Jesus that my friends and the many Jesuits I have known over the years have given me. I thank especially the members of my community who have given me the space, tolerated my eccentricities and allowed me to spend the 'years and years of world without event' that have gone into writing this book. I thank in a special way Genevieve Tobin who brought her many gifts to the shaping of this book.

> *... for Christ plays in ten thousand places,*
> *Lovely in limbs, and lovely in eyes not his ...*
> (G. M. Hopkins)

INTRODUCTION

This book asks each of us a question that is central to the gospels, 'And you, who do you, say that I am?' It is a question that Jesus might put to us in a variety of ways such as, Who am I for you? How do you feel about me? How do you see yourself in relation to me? What does being a Christian mean for you?

As we are being asked about how we see Jesus we are also being asked about how we see ourselves in our relationship with him, whether we see ourselves positively or negatively, as significant or insignificant. This is a vital question and on how we answer it will depend how alive and happy we will be.

In response to his question Jesus wants us to learn to believe that he is the good news, or the love of God expressed in human terms, and that we are loved by him just as he is by his Father. 'As the Father has loved me, so I have loved you; abide in my love.' (Jn 15:9) When Jesus invites us to 'abide in' his love he wants us to immerse our whole person in it, body and soul, heart and mind. He wants us to believe in how immensely significant we are in his eyes.

However, if we are to believe that Jesus loves us this much, we must face the mysterious resistance that distorted images of Jesus and of ourselves put in the way of this belief. If we do not change these distorted images, much of Jesus' love and the intimacy and joy it draws us into will remain dormant. To arouse our awareness of how passionately, profoundly and personally we are loved, and to believe in it, we will give a lot of attention to the practice of reflection and prayer. These have been found to be the best way to change how we see and feel about Jesus so that we might believe that we are loved by him as he is by his Father.

CHAPTER 1

Three answers to a crucial question

David Lodge's novel, *How Far Can You Go?*, tells the story of a number of Catholic students who were at university together in the early 1950s. As their story unfolds we see what being a Catholic meant for them then and how they saw themselves as different from other students. What made them different was primarily their adherence to a strict body of rules and ritual which they observed out of fear, especially of going to hell. Lodge describes how their attitudes changed as they went their separate ways after they finished their studies, got jobs and married. Even though as Catholics they all retained some common attitudes, a wide divergence in these appeared so that we have a reflection among them of the wide range of answers people gave to what being a Christian meant at that time. As we are exposed to the answers they gave we are being asked where we stand in relation to Jesus' central question in the gospels: 'And you, who do you say that I am?'

This question invites us to reflect on how we think of and feel about Jesus and about what he wants to do in our lives. In spite of the fact that our response to Jesus differs from person to person, and keeps changing throughout each person's life, there are three responses that are prevalent. These three responses are determined largely by three images of God and of Jesus which we are all heir to.

1) A judgemental Jesus
The first image is that Jesus, like God, is one who rewards and punishes. This image is prominent among the prophets and in the psalms and we see it too, for example, in the parable of the judgement in chapter 25 of Matthew's gospel. This image of Jesus was very prominent before the Second Vatican Council. It

is the image which dominates the lives of the young people at the beginning of David Lodge's novel. It was sustained, for example, by the parish mission with its stress on the four last things: death, judgement, heaven and hell. Underlying the prominence of this image was the belief that the best means of improving people's lives as Christians was through the principle of correction. This often involved inducing a strong element of fear to get people to obey the laws of God and of his church. Having lived a lot of my life with this model of growth, I can say that it made what was wrong very prominent and I easily became conscious of this in Jesus' presence. My initial reaction to the word of God was to search for its meaning and especially for its implications for living. As a result, my experience of every gospel story was of having a standard raised before me, a standard I usually felt I did not measure up to. Meeting Jesus in this context meant meeting someone who tended to be seen as judgemental and demanding.

Having worked on giving retreats for seven years during the 1980s, I became conscious of how dominant this image of a judgemental and demanding Jesus still was. I also became conscious of how unhealthy was the fear which this image of Jesus generated. The people who came on these retreats wanted to put things right between themselves and God, but the prospect of meeting and being with God in the retreat generated a lot of fear. Judging from the number of times in the Bible that God asks us not to be fearful in his presence, it is abundantly clear how unhealthy this kind of fear is and how much God wants to release us from its grip.

The image of Jesus as judgemental is likely to present itself in our experience in very subtle forms. For example, when we meet Jesus in the scenes of the gospel story we may see him as tending to give us advice or as being more concerned with the way things ought to be in our lives than with appreciating how good things already are. Jesus may also seem to be so far above the ordinary circumstances in which we live that he becomes what is called 'Pedestal Jesus'. We may as a result find it hard to be intimate with him or to let him become the friend he wishes to be. (Jn 15:15) Again, we may tend to cast Jesus in the role of an authority figure and feel uncomfortable in his presence, especially if we associate authority figures more with being corrected than with being affirmed.

2) Jesus loves us as part of a group

In the Second Vatican Council there was a dramatic change in the image of Jesus which was presented to us. In the council documents, especially in those dealing with the church and with lay people, there was a return to an image of Jesus which was dominant in the early church. There the stress is on the role which Jesus has within the Trinity and in their plans for our salvation. The emphasis is on Grace as what God plans to do in our lives, more than on God's will interpreted as what we are meant to do for God.

This image of Jesus had begun to take shape before the Council. It emerged at a popular level in people's devotion to the Sacred Heart and at a more theoretical level in the way this devotion was given theological backing in the encyclical on the Sacred Heart and in a new christology that was emerging in theology. Devotion to the Sacred Heart re-emphasised the fact that the primary concern of the Incarnation is the manifestation of God's love for us in the heart of Jesus. Theology for its part emphasised the reality that what is central to the Christian life is the fact that God is love and that in Jesus this love is revealed in a human way. (Jn 1:18)

Apart from supporting the influence of popular movements like devotion to the Sacred Heart, the change in the church's image of Jesus has remained largely theoretical. No adequate way has been found to popularise the new image of Jesus. Most people have, therefore, remained with what has been termed 'the simple faith of ordinary people'. This concept of faith finds expression in fidelity to the 'will of God', understood as fidelity to the ritual and rules the church has laid down for our observance.

This focus on the observance of rules led to an impersonal way of relating with Jesus. The gospels were approached as though they were a mere record of Jesus' life and of his message. Looked at in this way, the gospels become a biography of Jesus in which we experience him in an indirect way. This is like coming to know about someone but never meeting him or her personally. With this approach Jesus is seen as communicating with us only as members of a group such as the church so that our relationship with him becomes like that of the Israelites with God. They kept God at a distance and transferred responsibility for relating with him directly onto Moses. 'You speak to us, and we will listen; but do not let God speak to us, or we will die.' (Ex 20:18-21)

3) 'He loved me and sacrificed himself for me'

A third way of answering Jesus' question, 'And you, who do you say that I am?' is the subject matter of the rest of this book so we will just mention it here. This third way of responding to Jesus is inspired by the reality that he is the revelation of God's love for each person. He reveals it directly and personally, calling each of us by name into an intimate relationship with him. 'He calls his sheep by name and leads them out.' (Jn 14:9)

When Jesus calls each of us into this profound relationship, he is fulfilling the New Covenant announced by the prophet Jeremiah in which it was promised that we would all know God 'the least of us no less than the greatest'. (Jer 31:34) Jesus sees this most profound, intimate and personal revelation of God's love as his life's work. 'I have made your name known to them, and I will make it known, so that the love with which you have loved me may be in them, and I in them. (Jn 17:26)

CHAPTER 2

Jesus is the love of God

After a lifetime of reflection on Jesus' question, 'And you, who do you say that I am?' John summarises his answer in the first chapter of his gospel where he says, 'And the Word became flesh and lived among us, and we have seen his glory, the glory as of a father's only son, full of grace and truth.' (Jn 1:18) In other words, by becoming a human being Jesus embodied all the love which God essentially is, the reality that 'God is love'. (1 Jn 4:16) It is, however, in his death, or in his love of us 'to the utmost extent' (Jn 13:1), that the full range and depth of Jesus' love is revealed, how passionate it is and how passionately he wants to reveal it. 'We know love by this, that he laid down his life for us.' (1 Jn 3:16) To make the extraordinary array of love that we find in Jesus more real and credible we will look at nine aspects of this love that we develop as we make our way through the three ages of our lives, through the age of affection, of passionate love and of friendship.

The age of affection

As children especially but all through our lives as well we are very dependent on receiving four kinds of love that we call affection. These are the love of acceptance, of appreciation, of concern and of being acknowledged as significant. These four act as a foundation on which we build all the other loves and relationships we develop in life.

We experience people's love in a very concrete way when we are *accepted* by them in spite of our limitations. Being accepted allows us to see our human poverty in perspective or as a small part of our essential goodness. We see Jesus' acceptance and how constructive it is in the way he relates with Zacchaeus; there is no word of criticism even though most people thought of Zacchaeus as a sinner. Jesus helps him to accept himself as an essentially good person, one with whom Jesus was glad to associate. (Lk 19:5-6)

Appreciation is another fundamental way we experience love. When people highlight the good they find in us, they enliven us in the way Jesus does when he shows his appreciation of Zacchaeus' goodness. Where Jesus highlights the fact that Zacchaeus is 'a descendant of Abraham' the crowd highlight the fact that he is a sinner. (Lk 19:7-10)

People who show their love by their practical *concern* for our welfare have a powerful influence on us. Their belief in us, and in all we are capable of becoming, helps us to believe in ourselves. The concern Jesus showed for the Samaritan woman he met at the well had an extraordinary effect on her; she is profoundly influenced by his belief in her. Where she was an outcast who had to come to the well on her own she now becomes the person who seeks to draw her whole village into the relationship Jesus has drawn her into. (Jn 4:28-30)

We experience people's love when they *acknowledge* us or when, as well as accepting our weaknesses, they show their appreciation of our strengths and are concerned for our welfare. By this kind of sensitivity and respect, people give us a sense of being significant or worthwhile in their eyes. We see how Jesus acknowledges a person like the woman in Simon's house in the way he is sensitive to her loving gesture of washing his feet and in his respect for the essential goodness that her way of relating with him manifests. (Lk 7:44-47)

The age of passionate love
The age of affection, when we learn what is like to be accepted and appreciated by our parents, acts as a foundation for the age of passionate love when we learn to love others as we have been loved. We experience this dramatic shift from the love we receive to the love we want to give when we fall in love and another person becomes the centre of our world. We see this passionate love of Jesus in the way he loves us to 'the utmost extent' (Jn 13:1) and when he describes his life in terms of his passion to make his love known to us. (Jn 17:26) He comes to kindle the fire

of his love in people's hearts and he is prepared to 'be baptised' or immersed in the suffering which he knows will be involved in doing this. 'I came to bring fire to the earth, and how I wish it were already kindled! I have a baptism with which to be baptised, and what stress I am under until it is completed!' (Lk 12:49-50) The passion of Jesus to make his love known to us leads him to share not just all he has but all he is in the love he calls friendship.

The age of friendship
The fulfilment of passionate love is found in friendship when we become capable of sharing our inmost self with another or of giving another the gift of ourselves in self-disclosure. However, before this can happen, passionate love must become permanent and profound. When we fall in love we want our love to last and to deepen but whether it does so or not depends on how well we learn to accept each other's weaknesses and to appreciate each other's strengths. We all long to be accepted and appreciated in this way but the price of this is that we must reveal ourselves to another and to do this we must first come to know ourselves. For Jesus friendship consists in making ourselves known to others in as profound a way as possible. He spends his life revealing himself to us, sharing 'everything he has heard from his Father', their love, their union and their joy. This for Jesus is what friendship consists in (Jn 15:15) and, from the beginning of his life to its end, his main concern is to make 'everything he has heard from his Father known to us'. (Jn 1:18-17:26)

The Enneagram
In the exploration of these different kinds of love, which we come to know as we pass through these three ages of love, the Enneagram has had a major influence. In its extraordinarily perceptive description of nine types of human personality it provides a framework within which we can explore the extent and depth of Jesus' love. The part of the Enneagram we will be focussing on is what it calls the Divine Ideas. These are nine aspects of the love we receive and return within the main relationships we are engaged in during our lives. Our main interest in these Divine Ideas is that they may help us to clarify and define nine aspects of the love of God which Jesus seeks to reveal to us.

Without the very experiential knowledge that the Divine Ideas supply, the portraits of Jesus' love may remain too abstract or spiritual to be relevant to our everyday experience. Because the Divine Ideas are based on our experience of the people we know well, they provide a perceptive and realistic picture of the various features of these nine portraits of Jesus' love. As the Divine Ideas are so close to our experience of people we know, they provide us with a picture of human and divine love that is invaluable.

An outline of the nine portraits
What characterises the first portrait is Jesus' power to accept our weakness and infidelity in a way that is truly life-giving. The second portrait is of affection, especially that which appreciates and delights in us. The love depicted in the third portrait of Jesus is very practical in its concern that our dream might be realised to the full. The fourth portrait is of how personal Jesus' love is, how he relates with people one to one, always being sensitive to where they are and respectful of the unique character of each person he meets.

In the fifth portrait of Jesus we meet a person who loves us so profoundly that he shares with us not just all he has but all he is in making himself known to us. The sixth portrait focuses on the fidelity of Jesus and how permanent his love is in spite of our infidelity. What is most distinctive about the seventh portrait is the happiness it depicts. In this portrait Jesus is full of the joy of the Spirit and wishes to share with us this joyful attitude to life. The eight portrait is of Jesus as a person who is passionate about life. This is particularly true in his death and resurrection where he loves us 'to the utmost extent'. What characterises the ninth portrait of Jesus is the love of friendship which Jesus initiates by giving us a gift of himself in self-disclosure.

CHAPTER 3

Expressing God's love in human terms

If we are to appreciate the diversity and depth of the divine love which we looked at in Chapter 2, we must allow it to become incarnate or be revealed to us in human terms. This is what the Great Commandment invites us to do when it challenges us to be loved and to love with our 'whole heart and soul, mind and strength'. We assume here that 'heart, soul, mind and strength' correspond to the four levels at which we relate. In other words we take in love and return it with our body's senses and our heart's feelings, with our soul's capacity to glimpse the significance of what happens and our mind's capacity to form convictions of what is true and worthwhile in life. (Lk 10:25-28) It is in getting our whole person involved in Jesus' love in this way that we 'abide in' his love and enjoy the fullness of life and happiness he wants for us. (Jn 15:9-11)

Four levels at which we relate
1) When Jesus becomes a human being and takes on a body like ours, he seeks to communicate with us through our *senses*. That we allow him to do so is important because what we see, hear, touch, taste and smell is basic to the way we know another person. It is in the body and its senses that we lay the foundation of the rest of our experience. For example, as infants we take in love mainly through our experience of being touched.

2) Our *feelings*, which are aroused by what we hear people say or see them do, are often neglected. This is partly because we believe that our feelings are not important, whereas they play a key role in the way we relate. If we are to know Jesus, we cannot afford to neglect our feelings as they are a unique source of an intimate knowledge of him. This knowledge, that the heart has access to, depends on our being able to notice, name and share our feelings.

3) If we feel deeply about something that happens, it means that it is saying something significant to us and it is the role of *intuition* to notice and articulate this. Becoming aware of and learning to trust this capacity for intuition is an essential part of coming to know Jesus. For example, we learn what love is like from the glimpses of it we get from people like our family and friends, and these glimpses, though of a limited human love, are valuable intimations of the love of Jesus. They make his love real for us.

4) If we are to make our own of these intimations of the love of Jesus which people give us, we need to make use of our capacity for raising these glimpses which we get of ourselves and of others to the level of convictions. Changing these glimpses of what is true and worthwhile in life into convictions is the function of the deepest level of our experience. It is at this convictional level of our experience that we seek to assimilate the fruit of our sensate, feeling and intuitive experiences so that we believe in it.

There is an inbuilt interdependence between all the levels of our experience through which Jesus makes his love known to us. From what we sense and feel we get glimpses or impressions of what the love of Jesus is like. It is when these glimpses become convictions that our whole person is engaged in the love of Jesus and that we allow the word to become flesh and dwell in us. (Jn 1:14)

If we neglect any of these ways we come to know Jesus, our knowledge of him may become too intellectual and spiritual to engage our whole person. For example, we have tended to stress Jesus' divinity to the near exclusion of his humanity, with the result that we may not allow him to become a human being in a real sense because many of the ways he wants to reveal himself to us in human terms have not been developed. We need to find some way of arousing all this potential we have to relate with him in the truly human way that his Incarnation makes possible.

Significant People
There are those in our lives, like our parents, the person we marry, our family and our friends, who have influenced us deeply and have become what are called significant people. Their significance springs from the fact that they give us a tangible

and engaging impression of what love, and thus what God, is like. In this sense they continue the work of the Incarnation for, though their love is limited, they open our hearts to different experiences of love to which Jesus can then speak. We have a great need to return to those people who believe in us and to arouse our dormant memories of the ways they have acknowledged, accepted and affirmed us. To leave these memories in their dormant state is to be out of touch with 'the riches of his glorious inheritance among the saints.' (Eph 1:17-18) 'Human love is the instrument we can use to explore the mystery of love which God is.' (Jack Dominian)

Our underground stream of our inner wisdom
We can compare the dormant experience of the ways we have been loved by significant people to an underground stream of inner wisdom. It is an underground stream in the sense that it runs well below the surface of our consciousness. In this stream, that runs from one end of our life to the other, we have a huge accumulation of wisdom, or a lifetime's experience of being loved, that is rooted in the love of God that the Spirit seeks to give us an interior knowledge of. Since the Spirit has been teaching us throughout our lives there is a record written in our bodies and souls, in our minds and hearts of how the love of Jesus has evolved in us. This record is unique to each person, with the result that nobody but ourselves can get in touch with and take responsibility for exploring our inner wisdom. Becoming aware and making the best use of our dormant inner wisdom is a difficult task for it involves learning the art of reflection and prayer which we will examine in Chapter 5. Before we do that, we need to examine why we have such difficulty doing what we are made for, which is to answer the essential call of Jesus to believe in the good news of God's love and providence.

CHAPTER 4

Why do we not believe the good news?

Our reluctance to take the necessary steps to believe the good news is a problem that has puzzled Christians from earliest times. In general the reason for this reluctance is that there is another voice besides that of Jesus which we tend to believe in. This is the voice of an illusion about ourselves, created by our tendency to let the small fraction of ourselves that is weak and wayward capture our attention and dominate what we see. This illusion then obscures or blocks the vision of ourselves which Jesus wants us to believe in. 'For the fascination of evil obscures what is good.' (Wis 4:12)

There are a number of sources of this illusion but two basic ones: the growth of a distorted image of ourselves and of Jesus. The growth of these is so subtle and gradual that it takes hold of our mind and heart before we notice what is happening. Initially, the illusion about ourselves results from strong negative feelings such as anger, guilt or fear. For example, when we get upset about something, the negative feelings this gives rise to can dominate our attention and create the illusion that an experience was bad when in fact it was mainly good. If these strong negative feelings which this gives rise to keep recurring, they can colour the way we see ourselves. If we often find ourselves in an ugly mood, we can easily begin to identify with it so that it can create the prevailing image we have of ourselves. If this image is allowed to grow unchecked, it can easily erode our positive self-image and even replace it with a negative one.

This poor self-image can in turn makes it difficult for us to believe. No matter how persuasively people, and particularly Jesus, tell us good things about ourselves we deny them or cut them down to a size that we are comfortable with. When our poor self-image becomes well established and deeply felt it makes the affirmation or good news which the gospel asks us to believe seem unreal. Nothing Jesus says to us about loving us 'just as' the Father loves him (Jn 15:9) can gainsay the persuasive voice of the deeply ingrained conviction that we are not lovable. Jesus compares these distorted images to seven evil spirits that take possession of us and that we find it extremely difficult to rid ourselves of. (Lk 11:24-26)

Illusions we have about Jesus

The second basic reason why we resist the love of Jesus is the distorted images we have of him. It is important that we recognise these images because if we are not aware of their influence they can impair our relationship with Jesus and our ability to hear his 'good news'. We will look at two of these distorted images and the ways they may damage our relationship with Jesus.

The image of Jesus as *judgemental* often arises from our belief that the best way to help people to grow is to correct what is wrong in their lives. If we approach the gospels believing that Jesus fosters our growth in this way, we are likely to focus on the meaning and implications of each story we find there. The effect of this is that each story in the gospels puts up a standard before us and asks us how we are measuring up to it. If our answer usually is that we are not meeting these standards, we will experience feelings of guilt and these will confirm our poor self-image.

Another distorted image of Jesus is that he is *demanding*. An example of this is the Great Commandment that is central to Jesus' teaching. When in it we hear Jesus saying to us that we must love the Lord our God with our whole heart, our whole soul, our whole mind and our whole strength, this may appear to be an unrealistic demand. This is especially true when we consider our past performance and how half-hearted we often are in our response to this commandment.

We may also associate the image of a demanding Jesus with the idea of the will of God. When I was young I used to hear my parents speak of the will of God especially in connection with difficult things that we had to do or with heavy burdens we had to bear. So I grew up with a sense of a relentless will of God that often seemed to be indifferent to our personal desires and feelings. I felt that if I got close to God or Jesus they would make demands and that these would be made irrespective of my own desires and plans.

Jesus works out a plan

Jesus has a plan to free us from the illusions that make it difficult for us to believe in his love. This plan is that under the Spirit's guidance we would come to know him and the love he has for us. The basic response that Jesus calls for is that we would believe the good news or the revelation of God's love that it is Jesus' lifelong ambition to make known. 'I made your name known to them, and I will make it known, so that the love with which you have loved me may be in them, and I in them.' (Jn 17.26) If we are to believe in this love we need to repent or undertake the change of mind and heart that is called for if we are to accept the radically new vision of himself and of ourselves that Jesus asks us to make our own of. One of the most effective ways of answering this essential Christian call is by listening and responding to what Jesus reveals to us. This conversation with Jesus, that St Augustine saw as the essence of prayer, will be the subject matter of the next chapter.

CHAPTER 5

Coming to know Jesus: an exercise

'The most important fact in all of theology and spirituality
is that the three persons of the Trinity
want to reveal themselves to each person.'
(Karl Rahner)

The way of praying we will focus on in this chapter is a practical response to the passionate desire of the three persons of the Trinity to reveal themselves to each of us. It is a response to how the Spirit, in every gospel story, wishes to lead us into 'all the truth' or into the love of the Father that Jesus expresses in human terms. You can use the following steps to answer Jesus' invitation to 'abide in' his love or to immerse your whole person, body and soul, heart and mind in it. 'As the Father has loved me, so I have loved you; abide in my love.' (Jn 15:9-11)

1. Quieten yourself in whatever way you wish, such as by listening to the sounds you hear around you. Then focus your attention on the Trinity's presence by repeating a word or phrase that helps you to do this.

2. Read a gospel story and notice what aspect of Jesus' love it reveals to you. Choose a word or a phrase to express this love and then savour it by repeating the word or phrase. For example, you might notice that Jesus is kind, sensitive or puts himself out for people.

3. Spend time letting the attractiveness of this aspect of Jesus' love engage you with the glow or beauty inherent in all love. This attractiveness is revealed in the way Jesus looks at or treats someone in the story, in the style or artfulness with which he relates. As we saw in Chapter 3, it is a great help to ponder the way someone you know reveals this kind of love and its attractiveness to you.

4. Put words on what, in effect, Jesus is saying to someone in the gospel story and then let him say these words to you. The more challenging and personal the words you choose are the better. Let Jesus say these words to you a number of times to let the love they express and its attractiveness sink in.

5. Tell Jesus how you feel about what he says to you. You may find that one part of you resists this while another part welcomes it with gratitude, hope or joy.

Reflecting on your prayer
The purpose of reflection is to become aware of the fact that the Father, Jesus and their Spirit reveal themselves to you in prayer. It is also meant to help you to become familiar with the signs of how they want to do this by means of the Spirit enlightening your mind and attracting your heart. The Spirit will always be highlighting some aspect of Jesus' love and attracting you with its radiance. Therefore, when you reflect on your prayer, dwell with the reality that it is the Spirit who leads you into an intimate knowledge of the love of God she has poured into your heart. Then, notice and record, however briefly, anything that struck you about this love during the prayer. For example:
– what aspect of Jesus' love you stayed with,
– what you found attractive about this love,
– what words Jesus used to express this love to you,
– how you felt about this love and its attractiveness.

Begin your next period of prayer by reading what you have written. This will give continuity and lead to a build-up of what is being revealed to you about Jesus' love. From this a true vision of who Jesus is for you and who you are for Jesus will take shape. In this way you will be answering the question he asks you each day: 'And you, who do you say that I am?'

> Let us hang upon the lips of the faithful
> For the Spirit of God is upon every one of them.
> *(Paulinus of Nola)*

'A new and radiant vision of your glory'
The following is an outline of the way the nine portraits of Jesus will be presented in this book. We will approach them as nine portraits of Jesus' love and its glory we wish to paint. On the

first page of each portrait we will sketch an outline of our personal experience of people who have given us some impression of the various features of the portrait. Doing this gives us a feel for the features within our own experience before we look at the way they are painted for us in the gospels. On the second page of each portrait we will look at how its main features are interrelated so that we might catch a glimpse of the glory of God revealed in the face of Jesus.

We will then fill in the features of each portrait. At the beginning of each of these features we will return to some area of our personal experience which is particularly relevant to the feature with a view to making it more real and engaging. We will then fill in the detail of each feature from what is recorded in the four gospels. Our ultimate objective is to see a vision of Jesus' love and to be enraptured by its glory. This love and its attractiveness draws us into an environment in which we can experience Jesus' own joy in all its fullness. 'I have said these things to you so that my joy may be in you, and that your joy may be complete.' (Jn 15:11)

In the wonder of the incarnation
your eternal Word has brought to the eyes of faith
a new and radiant vision of your glory.
In him we see our God made visible
and so are caught up in the love of the God we cannot see.
(Preface of Christmas 1)

The life-giving love of Jesus

This portrait is of a love that is *life-giving*. The people who image this kind of love for us are those who are full of life themselves and who want us also to live it to the full. They do this by encouraging us to face two important realities: the fact that we are weak and wayward and the fact that we are gifted and graced. They urge us to face our potential as well as our poverty in such a way that we do not get so caught up in what is defective that we are unable to appreciate what is good.

There are three features of this first portrait that are particularly life-giving. The first of these is experienced in those people who *accept us as we are* and the second emerges in their *appreciation* of our goodness. These two life-giving features are balanced by a third. This is people's *concern* that we would become aware of and take responsibility for realising our potential to the fullest extent.

The people who manifest to us this life-giving love are *idealistic* in wanting us to live life ever more fully. Their idealism or concern for all we yet might be does not obscure their view of all the good that is already present in us. Their idealism is thus balanced by a healthy *realism* so that they do not engage in excessive striving to eradicate our defects.

The people who reflect the love we are considering in this portrait have *perspective*. They keep their eye on what is essential and on how all else is related to this. Because they have this broad vision they can live contentedly with what is defective as they see this as only a small part of a largely gifted and graced self. There is a *serenity* about this portrait that grows out of the balance we find in people who have learned to live with their weaknesses and their strengths, with their idealism and their realism, and with the perspective this gives them.

The features of the first portrait of Jesus

1. Jesus loves us in a *life-giving* way to the degree that he shares with us the life he enjoys with his Father. This life is experienced in practice as an interior knowledge of how Jesus accepts and affirms us.

2. A key feature of this portrait of Jesus is the way he *accepts* the limited and sinful side of us. He identifies with our weaknesses, sees them in perspective and delights in our efforts to deal with them.

3. What gives Jesus this perspective is his *appreciation* of and even his delight in us. This is based on the fact that he loves us just as his Father does him. He spends his life fostering our faith in this reality.

4. Jesus is *concerned* that we would realise the dream that coming to know him and his Father's love fulfils for us. His concern is balanced with a deference that leaves us free to be ourselves.

5. The *idealism* of Jesus is based on an idea of perfection that is not an achievement but a gift given. Through this gift we can come to know Jesus' love and the life in abundance this brings us.

6. Jesus' idealism is balanced by a forthright *realism* that allows him to forgive our neglect of or indifference to his gift. In spite of our infidelity he retains a sense of our essential goodness.

7. Jesus, by balancing his idealism and his realism, is a person with *perspective*. He keeps before him a vision of his Father's love as what is central to life and sees all in the light of this.

8. The *serenity* of Jesus springs from the way he balances idealism and realism. By appreciating our strengths and accepting our weaknesses, he lives contentedly with the weeds amid the wheat.

FEATURE 1

One who is really alive

Before we look at what Jesus means by *being really alive,* it might be worthwhile to look at what people today understand when they talk about living life to the full. Some people may interpret leading a full life in material terms and associate it with having a good standard of living. Other people may be prepared to sacrifice a degree of prosperity in order to adopt a simpler lifestyle lived in a healthy environment. Life for others may be associated with good relationships with family, friends and colleagues. Again, some people may think of life in terms of the love they have received and given in their relationships with the significant people of their lives. Then again some may include in their idea of a full life a spiritual dimension such as Jesus' belief that the one who believes 'has eternal life'. (Jn 5:54)

The first feature of this portrait of Jesus reveals a person who is fully alive and comes to share his life with us in all its abundance. 'I came that they may have life, and have it abundantly.' (Jn 10:10) In John's gospel Jesus tells us in very simple terms what life is all about for him:

> 'And this is eternal life, that they may know you, the only true God, and Jesus Christ whom you have sent.' (Jn 17:3)

When Jesus uses the word *know* to explain what he means by life, he is speaking about an interior knowledge of being loved by God and of returning that love. When he is asked what we must do to share this life he offers us, he says that we must keep his commandments.

> Just then a lawyer stood up to test Jesus. 'Teacher,' he said, 'what must I do to inherit eternal life?' He said to him, 'What is written in the law? What do you read there?' He answered, 'You shall love the Lord your God with all your heart, and with all your soul, and with all your strength, and with all your mind; and your neighbour as yourself.' And he said to him, 'You have given the right answer; do this, and you will live.' (Lk 10:25-28)

Seeing life within the context of the commandments means that for Jesus life involves getting our whole person engaged in being loved and in loving within the main relationships of life. To grasp in a concrete way how life-giving is the love Jesus is talking about here we need to draw on our experience of a number of aspects of it which we are familiar with. We will look more closely at these aspects of love in later features so it will suffice here to introduce them.

There is first of all a love Jesus shows us when he *accepts* us with all our limitations and sinfulness much as he accepted the woman in Simon's house. He is at home with her rather than being embarrassed by her gestures of intimacy in front of a critical crowd. Again he shows his love for her by his *appreciation* of her goodness seen in her courtesy towards him. His *concern* for her is also obvious in the way he is anxious to restore her dignity before Simon and his guests who are ashamed of her. Finally, Jesus *acknowledges* her or restores her sense of worth and importance so that she must have left Simon's house with a renewed sense of her dignity.

One of the Pharisees asked Jesus to eat with him. And a woman in the city, who was a sinner, having learned that he was eating in the Pharisee's house, brought an alabaster jar of ointment. She stood behind him at his feet, weeping, and began to bathe his feet with her tears and to dry them with her hair ... Now when the Pharisee who had invited him saw it, he said to himself, 'If this man were a prophet, he would have known who and what kind of woman this is who is touching him – that she is a sinner.' Jesus spoke up and said to him, 'Simon, I entered your house; you gave me no water for my feet, but she has bathed my feet with her tears and dried them with her hair ... Therefore, I tell you, her sins, which were many, have been forgiven; hence she has shown great love. But the one to whom little is forgiven, loves little.' And he said to the woman, 'Your faith has saved you; go in peace.' (Lk 7:36-50)

FEATURE 2

He is familiar with all our weakness

In this feature we look at how people, by accepting our weakness and waywardness, can teach us to deal with this side of ourselves in a constructive or life-giving way. This acceptance is a key feature of this portrait for unless we accept our weakness we will have difficulty contemplating the other features of this portrait. For example, if we are fixated with what is wrong in our lives, with our deficiencies, we will find it hard to accept the appreciation of others and their concern for us.

> A friend is one to whom one may pour out all the contents of one's heart, chaff and grain together, knowing that the gentlest of hands will take and sift it, keep what is worth keeping and with a breath of kindness blow the rest away. *(Arabian Proverb)*

Distinctive of this feature of Jesus' style of loving is his capacity to focus on what is good in people and to accept their shortcomings in the light of this. If we watch the way Jesus relates with Zacchaeus, we do not find him focusing on his deficiencies but rather on the good he finds in him.

> He entered Jericho and was passing through it. A man was there named Zacchaeus; he was a chief tax collector and was rich ... 'Zacchaeus, hurry and come down; for I must stay at your house today.' So he hurried down and was happy to welcome him. All who saw it began to grumble and said, 'He has gone to be the guest of one who is a sinner' ... Then Jesus said to him, 'Today salvation has come to this house, because he too is a son of Abraham. For the Son of Man came to seek out and to save the lost.' (Lk 19:1-10)

Jesus knows what the experience of our human limitations feels like and what it means to be immersed in our sinful world and its temptations. He can, therefore, identify with us in our experience of weakness and temptation and say to us no matter how we feel, 'I know how you feel for I have been there myself.'

Since, then, we have a great high priest who has passed

through the heavens, Jesus, the Son of God, let us hold fast to our confession. For we do not have a high priest who is unable to sympathise with our weaknesses, but we have one who in every respect has been tested as we are, yet without sin. (Heb 4:14-15)

This willingness of Jesus to immerse himself in our humanity, and especially in its weak and wayward side, is symbolised in the story of how Jesus cured a leper. It is an important dimension of this story that in Jesus' time lepers had to live outside the community and they were not allowed to approach healthy people, much less to touch or be touched by them. It is, therefore, very significant that the leper in Mt 8:1-3 feels free to approach Jesus and that Jesus touches him.

'There was a leper who came to Jesus and knelt before him, saying, "Lord, if you choose, you can make me clean." He stretched out his hand and touched him.'

In the parable of the Pharisee and the tax collector we see that Jesus feels at home with the tax collector while the self-righteous attitude of the Pharisee puts him beyond the reach of Jesus. (Lk 18:13-14)

We find a powerful revelation of this feature of Jesus in the way he deals with Peter's betrayal. What Peter had done was not held against him but he was even restored to the very special relationship he had with Jesus before he betrayed him.

'When they had finished breakfast, Jesus said to Simon Peter, "Simon son of John, do you love me more than these?" He said to him, "Yes, Lord; you know that I love you." Jesus said to him, "Feed my lambs".' (Jn 21:15)

It is in meeting Jesus as one who is happy to touch the leper in us, and even to embrace it, that we learn to embrace and to befriend this side of ourselves. We need to acknowledge that the treasure we possess is held 'in clay jars'. (2 Cor 4:6)

FEATURE 3

Jesus' appreciation of our goodness

Once we have adjusted to people's acceptance of the side of us that is limited and sinful, we become more open to listen to their affirmation. This affirmation is two-sided in that it highlights and appreciates all the good that is already ours just as it is concerned that we realise all our potential for life and happiness. In this feature we will look at how life-giving it is when people appreciate us, when they draw our attention to and help us own the unique goodness that belongs to each of us. This appreciation is an essential part of the love which gives us life and sustains it.

> Without affirmation, love does not exist. Permeated with a proper attitude concerning the value of a person – and such an attitude we termed affirmation – love reaches its fullness. Without this affirmation of the value of a person as a whole, love disintegrates and, in fact, does not exist at all. *(Karol Wojtyla)*

That Jesus believed in the life-giving power of appreciation is clear from the fact that he came to proclaim the good news that we are loved by Jesus as he is by his Father. (Mk 1:14-15) In his eyes therefore we are profoundly lovable, good and beautiful. 'As the Father has loved me, so I have loved you; abide in my love.' (Jn 15:9)

That Jesus is very appreciative of the goodness of those around him is clear from the way he deals with his disciples. In spite of their lack of faith and the fact that he knows they will desert and betray him, he chooses to highlight the reality that they are for the most part receptive of his revelation and believe in it. He also stresses the fact that he is glorified in them which means that they, like Jesus, show the radiance of the Father's love to the world.

> The words that you gave to me I have given to them, and they have received them and know in truth that I came from you; and they have believed that you sent me ... All mine are yours, and yours are mine; and I have been glorified in them. (Jn 17:8-10)

In the way that he deals with the woman in Simon's house, Jesus demonstrates his determination to highlight the good he finds in everyone and especially in those whom society is inclined to reject. In his consciousness of how lovable and loving this woman is he 'remembers her sins no more'. Like each one of us she is a 'sinner', a person with a dark side but it is as if Jesus does not notice this in his desire to highlight her goodness. What he does emphasise is all the signs of this goodness, how she washes his feet with her tears and dries them with her hair, how she kisses his feet and anoints them with precious ointment. (Lk 7:44-50)

Jesus' appreciation of the Roman centurion's faith is striking in that he belonged to a culture despised by the people Jesus moved among.

> 'When Jesus heard him, he was amazed and said to those who followed him, "Truly I tell you, in no one in Israel have I found such faith".' (Mt 8:5-10)

Jesus has such a high opinion of each person's greatness that he can say that 'the least in the kingdom of God is greater than John the Baptist'. (Mt 11:11) This greatness does not consist in power or achievement, nor does it consist in what we have or in striving to make ourselves great. Instead it is a dignity conferred on us by Jesus as a gift when he says that we are loved by the Father just as he is. (Jn 15:9) He longs that we would come to know this real source of our greatness, what he calls 'the gift of God'. (Jn 4:10)

What is very striking about Jesus' appreciation of each and every person, no matter what their background may be, is that he does not just appreciate the great things they may do periodically. As he did with the woman in Simon's house, Jesus highlights each person's most unobtrusive gestures and singles out for mention the simplest acts of kindness.

> 'For truly I tell you, whoever gives you a cup of water to drink because you bear the name of Christ will by no means lose the reward.' (Mk 9:41)

33

FEATURE 4

Jesus wants the very best for us

As well as being appreciative of all the good that we have already attained, those who affirm us are concerned that we attain all the good we are capable of. This concern is life-giving and we might go as far as Martin Heidigger the German philosopher who says we are constituted by those who are concerned about us. Each of us has a fund of personal experience of this concern in the intimate knowledge of how our family and friends want the best for us. People's concern is particularly life-giving when they are tuned in to where we are and to what we are ripe for or when their deep desire for all that is best for us does not hinder their deference for our freedom.

The miracles Jesus works are symbolic of his concern to heal the wounds from our past which each of us carries. In the following scene from the gospel Jesus is 'moved with pity' or 'filled with compassion' for a leper, for the deeply wounded person in each of us. We can sense the intensity of Jesus' concern in his words, 'Of course I want to.'

> A leper came to him begging him, and kneeling he said to him, 'If you choose, you can make me clean.' Moved with pity, Jesus stretched out his hand and touched him, and said to him, 'I do choose. Be made clean!' Immediately the leprosy left him, and he was made clean. (Mk 1:40-42)

In the parable of the banquet, we have a symbol of another aspect of Jesus' concern for us. This is his concern that we enter the intimate relationship he wants to initiate, establish and maintain with each one of us.

> Someone gave a great dinner and invited many ... Then the owner of the house said to his slave, 'Go out at once into the streets and lanes of the town and bring in the poor, the crippled, the blind, and the lame.' And the slave said, 'Sir, what you ordered has been done, and there is still room.' Then the master said to the slave, 'Go out into the roads and lanes, and compel people to come in, so that my house may be filled.' (Lk 14:15-24)

There is a delicate balance between being intensely concerned for the good of others and at the same time leaving them free to do what they think is best. It is easy to pressurise those we are deeply concerned about into following our plans and into realising these at the pace which we think is best for them. The way Jesus relates with the woman at the well is remarkable. He manifests his deep concern that she might 'know the gift of God' and he gently leads her on towards an experience of that gift. She is gradually and freely led on, firstly to become interested, then involved and finally to be so filled with enthusiasm that she brings her whole village out to meet Jesus.

> Many Samaritans from that city believed in him because of the woman's testimony, 'He told me everything I have ever done.' So when the Samaritans came to him, they asked him to stay with them; and he stayed there two days. And many more believed because of his word. They said to the woman, 'It is no longer because of what you said that we believe, for we have heard for ourselves, and we know that this is truly the Saviour of the world.' (Jn 4:39-42)

It is in the farewell discourse at the last supper that Jesus becomes most explicit about the exalted nature of his concern for us.

> 'The glory that you have given me I have given them, so that they may be one, as we are one, I in them and you in me, that they may become completely one, so that the world may know that you have sent me and have loved them even as you have loved me.' (Jn 17:22-23)

This concern of Jesus for us incorporates every area of our experience from the most mystical to the most ordinary and earthy.

> 'Are not five sparrows sold for two pennies? Yet not one of them is forgotten in God's sight. But even the hairs of your head are all counted. Do not be afraid; you are of more value than many sparrows.' (Lk 12:6-7)

FEATURE 5

The idealism of Jesus

We admire those who consistently do things well, people who have a passion for excellence. We admire this particularly when this passion for excellence is channelled into the way they relate. We admire those people too who have the capacity to bring the best out of others, not by constantly giving advice or raising the standards they expect them to meet but by a mixture of acceptance and appreciation; by a pedagogy of affirmation as opposed to one of correction.

The ideal which Jesus puts before us, such as his invitation to be as perfect as God is, may seem to us utopian in the far-from-ideal world in which we are immersed. We may, therefore, fail to be attracted by the ideal Jesus sets before us. However, if we see Jesus' ideal for us, not in terms of a perfection or an achievement on our part, but as a gift we are invited to make our own of, this will make all the difference. This is what Jesus longs for when he says to the Samaritan woman, 'If you only knew the gift of God.' (Jn 4:10) In the synoptic gospels this gift is spoken of as the 'good news' of God's love and providence and it is what we are essentially called to as Christians.

> The time is fulfilled, and the kingdom of God has come near; repent, and believe in the good news. (Mk 1:15) The Spirit of the Lord is upon me, because he has anointed me to bring good news to the poor. He has sent me to proclaim release to the captives and recovery of sight to the blind, to let the oppressed go free. (Lk 4:18)

Jesus' ideal or dream for us is that we would believe the good news of God's love that he portrays for us in his human person. Paul in his letter to the Ephesians expresses this ideal strikingly when he says that it consists in coming to know the full extent and depth of the love of Jesus so that we 'may be filled with all the fullness of God'.

> I pray that, according to the riches of his glory, he may grant that you may be strengthened in your inner being with power through his Spirit, and that Christ may dwell in your

hearts through faith, as you are being rooted and grounded in love. I pray that you may have the power to comprehend, with all the saints, what is the breadth and length and height and depth, and to know the love of Christ that surpasses knowledge, so that you may be filled with all the fullness of God. Now to him who by the power at work within us is able to accomplish abundantly far more than all we can ask or imagine, to him be glory in the church and in Christ Jesus to all generations, forever and ever. Amen. (Eph 3:16-21)

In Chapters 14-17 of his gospel, John tells of the dream Jesus has for us. It is that we would share in the love that the Father, Jesus and their Spirit have for each other and as a result that we would share in the 'complete' union and joy that the radiance of their love draws us into.

As the Father has loved me, so I have loved you; abide in my love. If you keep my commandments, you will abide in my love, just as I have kept my Father's commandments and abide in his love. I have said these things to you so that my joy may be in you, and that your joy may be complete. This is my commandment, that you love one another as I have loved you. No one has greater love than this, to lay down one's life for one's friends. You are my friends if you do what I command you. I do not call you servants any longer, because the servant does not know what the master is doing; but I have called you friends, because I have made known to you everything that I have heard from my Father. (Jn 15:9-15)

I speak these things in the world so that they may have my joy made complete in themselves ... The glory that you have given me I have given them, so that they may be one, as we are one, I in them and you in me, that they may become completely one, so that the world may know that you have sent me and have loved them even as you have loved me. (Jn 17:13, 22-23)

FEATURE 6

The realism of Jesus

We live out our ideals in a world where everyone is limited and sinful. To be a healthy realist we have to strike a balance between an idealism that does not face reality and a cynical attitude that drains us of the energy that our ideals should generate. It is difficult to get the balance right between challenging ourselves to take responsibility for realising our deep desires and on the other hand not setting our standards too high so that we get discouraged. We need to heed our inner voices urging us to follow our dream and at the same time not lose hope when faced with how little of our dream we are ready to realise at any stage of our journey.

God in making the prophet does not unmake the man. *(John Locke)*

The gospels paint a picture of Jesus as a person who is adept at balancing his idealism with the most down-to-earth realism. He never loses his idealism and enthusiasm in spite of the fact that he constantly faces indifference and hostility. He is at home with the very limited or even hostile response he gets to his efforts to help people. (Jn 7:1-13)

Jesus is well aware that there is little he can do with those who are out of sympathy with his ideals or with those who are wilfully blind to them. 'I came into this world for judgement so that those who do not see may see, and those who do see may become blind.' (Jn 9:39)

He feels strongly about this indifference to his cherished ideals and he expresses his frustration using very forthright imagery.

'Do not give what is holy to dogs; and do not throw your pearls before swine, or they will trample them under foot and turn and maul you.' (Mt 7:6)

Even though people are indifferent to and oppose Jesus in a very aggressive way, he never allows this dark area of his experience to get out of proportion. He has an extraordinary capacity to remain aware of the predominance of good in the world and to be patient with all the opposition to this good that is prevalent even among those closest to him.

> He put before them another parable: 'The kingdom of heaven may be compared to someone who sowed good seed in his field; but while everybody was asleep, an enemy came and sowed weeds among the wheat, and then went away. So when the plants came up and bore grain, then the weeds appeared as well. And the slaves of the householder came and said to him, 'Master, did you not sow good seed in your field? Where, then, did these weeds come from?' He answered, 'An enemy has done this.' The slaves said to him, 'Then do you want us to go and gather them?' But he replied, 'No; for in gathering the weeds you would uproot the wheat along with them. Let both of them grow together until the harvest; and at harvest time I will tell the reapers, "Collect the weeds first and bind them in bundles to be burned, but gather the wheat into my barn".' (Mt 13:24-30)

We see Jesus' flexibility in putting aside his plans or the ideal he has set himself in order to respond to the faith of the Canaanite woman. This contrasts with the inflexibility and hardheartedness of the scribes and the Pharisees. (Mk 7:24-30)

There is nothing of the narrow-minded or fanatical idealist in Jesus as he focuses on the good that others are doing even if they are not his disciples; he believes that 'whoever is not against you is for you.' (Lk 9:49-50)

Because Jesus sees people as predominantly good, he confronts those who bring to him the woman caught in adultery with the injustice of their attitude towards her. He does not condone her wrongdoing but he resists as unjust the hard-hearted and legal-minded attitude that renders her accusers insensitive to her essential goodness.

> 'Jesus straightened up and said to her, "Woman, where are they? Has no one condemned you?" She said, "No one, sir." And Jesus said, "Neither do I condemn you. Go your way, and from now on do not sin again".' (Jn 8:1-11)

FEATURE 7

Jesus: a person with perspective

The dictionary defines 'perspective' as the mental view of the relative importance of all things. Thus people with perspective have a broad view of things and are concerned with big issues. There is a tendency in human nature to lose touch with this broad vision and to become confined to a corner of life governed, for example, by material interests. In this way we allow our horizons of what is true and worthwhile to be narrowed rather than broadened.

Everyone takes the limits of his own field of vision for the limits of the world. *(Schopenhauer)*

When Jesus wants his disciples to see his sufferings and death in perspective he takes them up Mount Tabor where they are given a vision of him in all his glory. It is in the light of this that Jesus wants them to understand all that is happening in their lives. They are invited to see his suffering and death as the summation and climax of the story of God's love for them.

Now about eight days after these sayings Jesus took with him Peter and John and James, and went up on the mountain to pray. And while he was praying, the appearance of his face changed, and his clothes became dazzling white. Suddenly they saw two men, Moses and Elijah, talking to him. They appeared in glory and were speaking of his departure, which he was about to accomplish at Jerusalem. Now Peter and his companions were weighed down with sleep; but since they had stayed awake, they saw his glory and the two men who stood with him ... While he was saying this, a cloud came and overshadowed them; and they were terrified as they entered the cloud. Then from the cloud came a voice that said, 'This is my Son, my Chosen; listen to him!' (Lk 9:28-36)

In his second letter Peter tells us how the vision he was given on Tabor became for him a light in a dark world, and the context that gave him perspective for the rest of his life. (2 Pet 1:18-19)

People tend to keep alive the vision of reality on which they base their lives by constantly re-telling the story of how they were led to this vision or to see things in the way they do. For this reason Jesus gives us the Mass as a means of keeping alive a vision of reality at the centre of which is his love for us. We re-tell the story of the ultimate expression of this love in his passion and death.

> For I received from the Lord what I also handed on to you, that the Lord Jesus on the night when he was betrayed took a loaf of bread, and when he had given thanks, he broke it and said, 'This is my body that is for you. Do this in remembrance of me.' In the same way he took the cup also, after supper, saying, 'This cup is the new covenant in my blood. Do this, as often as you drink it, in remembrance of me.' For as often as you eat this bread and drink the cup, you proclaim the Lord's death until he comes. (1 Cor 11:23-26)

In the story of the two disciples on the road to Emmaus we have a practical example of how Jesus helps them to see their lives from the perspective of his love for them. He invites them to tell the story of their own sufferings and then he leads them to see their story within the much larger one of his own sufferings and death. When they hear his story depicted in the word of God they see all that had happened in the light of his love for them, especially in the light of the ultimate expression of this love in 'the breaking of bread'. When they see their lives from his perspective their desolation turns to consolation, their 'hearts burned within them as they listened to him on the way'. (Lk 24:30-32) We experience this perspective of Jesus when, like Paul, we come to know his love and evaluate everything in the light of it.

> 'I regard everything as loss because of the surpassing value of knowing Christ Jesus my Lord. For his sake I have suffered the loss of all things, and I regard them as rubbish, in order that I may gain Christ ' (Phil 3:8)

FEATURE 8

The serenity of Jesus

When we say that people are serene we mean that they are tranquil, unperturbed, calm and content. This serene disposition arises from a balance of a number of attitudes, from a mix of acceptance and appreciation, idealism and realism and especially from a sense of the relative importance of all things that seeing them in perspective gives us. Serenity is thus experienced as a contentment with the blend of good and bad, of potential and poverty that comprises each human life. We arrive at this contentment not through repressing our dark companion but by living contentedly with it and by seeing it in the light of all the good that is in us.

> God grant me the serenity to accept the things I cannot change, courage to change the things I can; and the wisdom to know the difference. *(Author unknown)*

The serenity of Jesus is a tranquillity or calmness we notice about him in the gospels. This is because he accepts and even identifies with the reality 'that he did not come to help angels' but became 'like his brothers and sisters in every respect'.

> For it is clear that he did not come to help angels, but the descendants of Abraham. Therefore he had to become like his brothers and sisters in every respect, so that he might be a merciful and faithful high priest in the service of God, to make a sacrifice of atonement for the sins of the people. Because he himself was tested by what he suffered, he is able to help those who are being tested. (Heb 2:16-18)

Jesus is not just content to live with our poverty but he sees it in the context of our goodness and our potential for goodness. We notice this contentment or serenity in the way he relates with people like the Samaritan woman (Jn 4), with Zacchaeus (Lk 19:1-13) and with the woman in Simon's house. (Lk 7:36-50) These people, who would have been seen by others as sinners and outcasts, represent that mixture of good and bad which we all are and which Jesus wants us to live serenely with in the way that he himself does.

The serenity of Jesus is closely linked with the contentment or happiness that he says belongs to the meek.

'Happy are the meek, for they will inherit the earth.' (Mt 5:5)

Jesus says that he would like us to learn this meekness from him and the serenity it brings with it. He says that this meekness brings us a share in his 'rest' which is closely related to the serenity we are contemplating in this feature.

'Take my yoke upon you, and learn from me; for I am gentle and humble in heart, and you will find rest for your souls.' (Mt 11:29)

As Isaiah prophesied, this gentle and serene attitude characterises the whole life of Jesus.

Here is my servant, whom I have chosen, my beloved, with whom my soul is well pleased. I will put my Spirit upon him, and he will proclaim justice to the Gentiles. He will not wrangle or cry aloud, nor will anyone hear his voice in the streets. He will not break a bruised reed or quench a smouldering wick until he brings justice to victory. And in his name the Gentiles will hope. (Mt 12:15-21)

The serenity of Jesus is most striking in his passion, death and resurrection. The description of these events in the gospels begins with the joyful scene of Jesus entering Jerusalem as its meek and humble king. 'Tell the daughter of Zion, Look, your king is coming to you, humble, and mounted on a donkey, and on a colt, the foal of a donkey.' (Mt 21:5) This image of Jesus as the serene king dominates the description of the events of his suffering, death and resurrection, especially in John's account of them.

'My kingdom is not from this world.' ... Pilate asked him, 'So you are a king?' Jesus answered, 'You say that I am a king. For this I was born, and for this I came into the world, to testify to the truth. Everyone who belongs to the truth listens to my voice.' (Jn 18:35-38)

The affection of Jesus

We have a lot of experience of affection, especially as it is experienced between parents and their children. One of the most positive qualities of this affection is that it leaves us *free* to be ourselves since genuine affection has not got to be earned but is there for us whether we respond to it or not. Affection is *the humblest of loves*, a reality we see in the way that parents provide the most menial services for their new-born child. Parents are sensitive to the needs of their children and can identify with them in their feelings and aspirations, in their joys and sorrows.

There are female and male characteristics of affection. Among the female ones are *compassion* and a *self-sacrificing generosity*. The compassionate aspect of affection is seen in the deep concern that inclines mothers especially to meet the needs and to share the pain of their children. The self-sacrificing generosity, which we associate especially with the affection of mothers, goes to endless rounds to cater for their children's needs and to realise their dreams.

There are two qualities that are associated with male affection, the first of which challenges us to *extend the horizons of our affection* by constantly broadening the circle of those we receive it from and share it with. We are challenged to let go of the comfortable confines to which we tend to limit our affection. The male quality of affection also challenges us to get our whole person involved in receiving and returning affection, our whole body and soul, our whole heart and mind.

The features of the second portrait of Jesus

1. In becoming a child and our brother Jesus invites us into a relationship of *affection* and into its capacity for appreciation and concern.

2. Whereas affection tends to attach strings to its love, that of Jesus leaves us *free* to do what we think best and feel up to. In this way Jesus is deferential in urging us to do what we are ripe for.

3. The affection Jesus shows us is *humble* in that greatness for him is in service. He enters our human poverty and invites us to find there the true greatness that is God's gift of grace.

4. Jesus in his affection is *sensitive* to our needs, feelings, weaknesses and gifts. His delayed response to our needs is not due to his lack of sensitivity but leaves room for our faith to grow.

5. In his affection for us Jesus is tender and *compassionate* in a world that is often aggressive and unfeeling. His compassion is illustrated in his parables of the good Samaritan and of the last judgement.

6. *Self-sacrificing generosity*, as it is portrayed for us in the parable of the good shepherd and above all in his death out of love for us, is distinctive of the Jesus' affection.

7. Jesus challenges us to believe that his *affection knows no bounds* and that it reaches out beyond family and friends to all equally.

8. Jesus also challenges us to let the full extent and depth of his affection *engage our whole person*, body and soul, heart and mind. This is the 'change of mind and heart' that belief in his love calls for.

FEATURE 1

Jesus as an affectionate person

Affection is a love experienced primarily within a family and especially between parents and their children. It is a love we are educated in at a time of life when we learn most of what we need to know about how to relate. Affection is our most formative experience of love because from our first moments we are surrounded by it and totally dependent on it. Though affection is of its nature inconspicuous, having little of the intensity of falling in love or the depth of friendship, it provides the foundation for all other forms of love.

> Affection is responsible for nine tenths of whatever solid and durable happiness there is in our natural lives. *(C. S. Lewis, Four Loves)*

The infancy stories in the gospels draw us into a relationship with Jesus where the dominant feature is affection. As we read through these stories given in Matthew (Mt 1:18-2:23) and Luke (Lk 1:26-2:52) it is interesting to notice how we are drawn into this relationship. As we contemplate these scenes we are presented with a person who is surrounded by the affection of Mary and Joseph and yet is vulnerable, humble and dependent.

> While they were there, the time came for her to deliver her child. And she gave birth to her firstborn son and wrapped him in bands of cloth, and laid him in a manger, because there was no place for them in the inn. (Lk 2:6-7)

Another way that Jesus leads us into a relationship of affection with him is by becoming our brother and one who is like us 'in every respect'. 'Go to my brothers and say to them, "I am ascending to my Father and your Father, to my God and your God".' (Jn 20:17) 'Therefore he had to become like his brothers and sisters in every respect.' (Heb 2:17) We are thus the members of Jesus' family and with him say to God, 'Abba! Father.'

> For those whom he foreknew he also predestined to be conformed to the image of his Son, in order that he might be the firstborn within a large family. (Rom 8:14-17, 29)

We are invited to enter fully into the warmth of our relationship as the brothers and sisters of Jesus by showing mutual affection.

> Love one another with mutual affection; outdo one another in showing honour. (Rom 12:10)

Another image of Jesus that calls for our affection is his depiction of himself as one who is at our service. This is a feature of the way parents show affection when they put themselves at the service of their children looking after their every need. Jesus often speaks of himself as fulfilling the role of the servant foretold by the prophet Isaiah, (Is 42:2-3) a role he assumed at his baptism and that he lived out in a life of inconspicuous service. 'Here is my servant, whom I have chosen.' (Mt 12:15-18)

If we are to be truly affectionate in our relationship with Jesus it is important that we work at allowing him to assume this role and be with us 'as one who serves'. We will have to work at this if we have a well established image of him as almost exclusively divine. The effect of this image which overemphasises his divinity is that we keep him at a respectful distance and do not accept the warmth of the affectionate relationship he wants to have with us.

> The greatest among you must become like the youngest, and the leader like one who serves. For who is greater, the one who is at the table or the one who serves? Is it not the one at the table? But I am among you as one who serves. (Lk 22:26-27)

Perhaps the most comprehensive picture of the affectionate nature of Jesus' love is seen in his meeting with the two disciples on the road to Emmaus. While the female quality of his affection appears in his sensitivity and compassion, the male quality comes across in the assertive way he challenges his disciples to understand their experience in a wider context. (Lk 24:17-19, Lk 24:25-27)

FEATURE 2

Free to give and not to give

The ideal of affection is that it is given freely with no strings attached. It is not possessive, as healthy affection leaves us free to come and go, to take wing after we have taken root. Genuine affection frees us to follow our own deep desires and does not insist that we meet other people's expectations or that we sacrifice our own interests to these.

> But the proper aim of giving is to put the recipient in a state where he no longer needs our gift. We feed children in order that they may soon be able to feed themselves; we teach them in order that they may soon not need our teaching.
> (C. S. Lewis, *Four Loves*)

The source of the freedom that characterises genuine affection is a sense of security arising from a conviction that our worth is guaranteed and we do not have to bid for it by doing things for others. This experience of affection frees us from the compulsive need to earn it, since it is a gift we have received from our family and friends.

Jesus believes that the source of his freedom and that which he would like us to enjoy is what he calls the truth.

> 'You will know the truth, and the truth will make you free.'
> (Jn 8:32)

The truth which is spoken about here is God's self-revelation as love in the person of Jesus. 'I am the truth.' (Jn 14:6) The fact that Jesus identifies with the truth makes him an eminently free person. This is because Jesus, being so conscious of being loved by his Father in such a profound way, is secure in that love and set free from the need to earn it. It is rarely we find someone so certain of being loved that he or she is not dominated by the need to earn it in all kinds of subtle ways.

Jesus wishes to share his freedom with us and thus the love he reveals has not got to be earned but only accepted. His love is thus essentially a gift given freely and unconditionally, with no strings attached; it is what he calls 'the gift of God'. (Jn 4:10)

This gift is not reserved for those whom Jesus calls the 'wise' and the 'intelligent'. It is not necessarily available to those who like the scribes and Pharisees are well versed in the law, but it is freely available to all who by their childlike attitude are open to receive it.

> I thank you, Father, Lord of heaven and earth, because you have hidden these things from the wise and the intelligent and have revealed them to infants; yes, Father, for such was your gracious will. (Lk 10:21-24)

One of the signs of the freedom Jesus enjoys is his willingness to share his life's work with us as he did with the seventy disciples he sent out. (Lk 10:1-2) He is even free enough to say that we will do even greater work than he does.

> Very truly, I tell you, the one who believes in me will also do the works that I do and, in fact, will do greater works than these, because I am going to the Father. (Jn 14:12)

It is a big temptation for those who care for others to continue to do for them what they should be encouraged to do for themselves. Genuine affection, however, gives people wings as well as roots. A sign of the freedom which Jesus enjoys is the fact that his affection is not possessive. He does not hold on to others in an excessively dependent way like one who needs to be needed to feel worthwhile. Jesus wants us to live with such an awareness of the 'kingdom of God' or of 'the gift of God' that we do not depend on outward possessions for our sense of worth. Like the seventy two that Jesus sent out, we are asked to offer others the gift of God and then leave them free to accept it or not. (Lk 10:8-11)

Jesus leaves us free to respond to him, if and when we are ready to do so, without putting pressure on us to move in the direction and at the pace he thinks best. It is striking how deferential Jesus is when the rich young man makes what Jesus knows to be a wrong decision. He respects his decision and does not pressurise him to sell what he has and to follow him. (Mk 10:17-23)

FEATURE 3

The humility of Jesus

> Affection, as I have said, is the humblest of loves. It gives it-
> self no airs. People can be proud of being 'in love' or of
> friendship. Affection is modest ... Affection lives with hum-
> ble, private things; soft slippers, old clothes, old jokes, the
> thump of a sleepy dog's tail on the kitchen floor, the sound of
> a sewing-machine, a golliwog left on the lawn. *(C. S. Lewis,*
> *Four Loves)*

What comes to mind when you hear the word humility? Is it an
invitation to face the truth about your weaknesses or is it mainly
about facing the reality of your strengths? In the past the word
humility brought to mind ideas of facing up to our inadequacies
as the main truth about ourselves we need to live with. Today
people are discovering that traditionally humility consisted in
facing the truth that we are not only limited and sinful beings
but that we are invited, in the words of the offertory prayer of
the Mass, 'to share in the divinity of Christ who humbled himself to share in our humanity'. So, for example, the author of *The*
Cloud of Unknowing distinguishes imperfect and perfect humility
in an enlightening way: 'The humility engendered by this experiential knowledge of God's goodness and love I call perfect ...
But the humility arising from a realistic grasp of the human condition I call imperfect.'

If we are accustomed to thinking of Jesus as being perfect, it may
not be easy to understand how he has cause to be humble and
how he can invite us to learn humility from him.

> Take my yoke upon you, and learn from me; for I am gentle
> and humble in heart, and you will find rest for your souls.
> (Mt 11:29)

The humility of Jesus is most obvious in his willingness to live
with the humanity he immersed himself in by his incarnation
and with the temptations that are a part of his being immersed
in the human condition. As a result, Jesus is one 'who in every
respect has been tested as we are, yet without sin.' (Heb 4:15)

Another image Jesus uses of the humility that is so central to his incarnation is that of becoming like a child. 'Whoever becomes humble like this child is the greatest in the kingdom of heaven.' (Mt 18:1-5) This image is often used by Jesus to portray the attitude adopted by those he calls 'the poor' in the beatitudes. It is an attitude Jesus identifies with when he says he is 'meek and humble of heart'. This means that Jesus adopts the position of a human being and faces the reality that he must depend on, trust in and surrender to who he is for his Father.

From the beginning of the gospel Jesus identifies with his role as the servant or son of God, the role which is implied in the words his Father addresses to him at his baptism. 'This is my Son (or servant), the Beloved, with whom I am well pleased.' (Mt 3:17) The qualities of the servant which Matthew finds most prominent in Jesus are that he is gentle and humble of heart.

> He will not wrangle or cry aloud, nor will anyone hear his voice in the streets. He will not break a bruised reed or quench a smouldering wick until he brings justice to victory. And in his name the Gentiles will hope. (Mt 12:15-21)

Jesus acts out this teaching on humility in a dramatic way when he washes his disciples' feet.

> So if I, your Lord and Teacher, have washed your feet, you also ought to wash one another's feet. For I have set you an example, that you also should do as I have done to you. (Jn 13:3-5, 12-15)

Jesus' humility is very apparent in the way that throughout his life he is with us 'as one who serves'. He symbolises this reality in the humble way he cares for us at the banquet he invites us to share with him.

> The greatest among you must become like the youngest, and the leader like one who serves. For who is greater, the one who is at the table or the one who serves? Is it not the one at the table? But I am among you as one who serves. (Lk 22:26-30, Jn 21:9-13)

FEATURE 4

The sensitivity of Jesus

When we reflect back on the way our parents showed us affection it is likely that their sensitivity to our needs, feelings and aspirations will stand out. Patrick Kavanagh, in the following lines from his poem *In Memory of My Mother*, captures this sensitivity when he recalls his own mother.

> You will have the road gate open, the front door ajar
> The kettle boiling and a table set
> By the window looking out at the sycamores –
> And your loving heart lying in wait
> You will know I am coming though I send no word

Yet, there are limits to the sensitivity of the best of parents as they often fail to heed their children's need to be listened to more and more as they mature. In their affection they may assume too readily that they know what is best and thus they may not listen to the aspirations of their children, especially when these differ from their own.

When we relate to Jesus we need to discern whether we experience him coming to us with his own agenda or whether he approaches us with great sensitivity to our personal views and aspirations. For example, when we hear Jesus speaking about the will of God we need to notice what this calls up for us. Does it call up the notion of meeting God's expectations regardless of our own, or whether we see God's will and our own deepest desires as similar or even identical?

In the incident where Jesus meets the widow at Nain he feels for her as she has lost her only son and is thus alone in the world. His feeling for her is conveyed by the sentence, 'He felt for her' or 'His heart went out to her.' This expression of Jesus' feeling is unusually strong for Luke who is reserved in reporting how Jesus felt. This dramatic expression of feeling is matched by the dramatic nature of the miracle he works. The story is symbolic of Jesus' sensitivity to each person's predicament.

When the Lord saw her, his heart went out to her and said,

'Do not weep.' Then he came forward and touched the bier, and the bearers stood still. And he said, 'Young man, I say to you, rise!' The dead man sat up and began to speak, and Jesus gave him to his mother. (Lk 7:13-15)

The scene in Mark's gospel in which Jesus answers Jairus' appeal for help also demonstrates his sensitivity to our desires and deep needs. It is significant that even though Jesus responds straight away to Jairus' need for help, he is interrupted on his way by the woman who suffers from incurable haemorrhaging. We may tend to interpret the delay of Jesus in answering Jairus' desperate cry for help as insensitivity when in fact it provided a space for Jarius' faith to grow and in this way to meet a deeper need than that of the cure of his son. We see how Jesus fosters this faith by protecting Jairus from the influence of the unbelieving crowd who pour scorn on Jesus' observation that the dead child is but asleep. After the sublime event where Jesus raises Jairus' daughter to life there is the very down-to-earth sensitivity of Jesus when he asks those standing around to give the child something to eat. (Mk 5:21-24, 35-43)

Jesus is sensitive to what is deepest in us and he invites us to tune in to and give expression to our desires, to our deepest longings, to our dream. We must do this realising two things: that we cannot realise our dream apart from God, and that God is passionate about realising the dream he built into us when he made us in his image.

Ask, and it will be given you; search, and you will find; knock, and the door will be opened for you. For everyone who asks receives, and everyone who searches finds, and for everyone who knocks, the door will be opened. (Mt 7:7-8)

We see a wonderful symbol of this desire of God to arouse our dream and to satisfy it in Mk 6:30-34.

FEATURE 5

The compassion of Jesus

Affection has a female as well as a male form of expression. Compassion and a self-sacrificing generosity characterise the female side while the male side is characterised by an affection that challenges us to broaden the horizons of our affection to include an ever wider world. Again the male side of affection challenges us to involve our whole person in it, our bodies and souls, our hearts and minds.

In this feature we will focus on the female characteristic of compassion. This is a feeling that flows from being sensitive to the difficulties others are experiencing and from a natural tendency to be concerned for them and to do something about their predicament. We see the compassion that characterised the life of Jesus in a number of images of him that we will just mention here as they will be developed more fully in other portraits of Jesus. There are images which have their origins in the Old Covenant and which Jesus adopts and develops in order to convey to us the extent and depth of his compassion. There is, for example, the image of the Servant (Mt 12:15-21) and of the good shepherd (Ezek 34, Jn 10:1-18) that Jesus builds on with ones like that of the good Samaritan. All these express in concrete terms the practical nature of Jesus' compassion.

> But a Samaritan while travelling came near him; and when he saw him, he was moved with pity. He went to him and bandaged his wounds, having poured oil and wine on them. Then he put him on his own animal, brought him to an inn, and took care of him.' (Lk 10:29-37)

In his dealings with people like the woman at the well (Jn 4) and with the two disciples on the road to Emmaus (Lk 24) there are powerful images of the range of Jesus' compassion, of how sensitive, warm and practical it is.

It is in the Beatitudes that we get our deepest insight into the compassion of Jesus for suffering humanity. The Beatitude which is most closely associated with this portrait of Jesus says,

> Blessed are the merciful, for they will receive mercy. (Mt 5:7)

It highlights Jesus' care, loving-kindness and compassion in a way that is further developed in Jesus' parables about the good Samaritan and the last judgement. Both these parables express the profound and practical concern of Jesus for wounded humanity.

> Come, you that are blessed by my Father, inherit the king-dom prepared for you from the foundation of the world; for I was hungry and you gave me food, I was thirsty and you gave me something to drink, I was a stranger and you wel-comed me, I was naked and you gave me clothing, I was sick and you took care of me, I was in prison and you visited me. (Mt 25:34-36)

In the light of these two parables what Jesus said in the Sermon on the Mount about the love that should characterise his follow-ers becomes a lot clearer.

> Do to others as you would have them do to you. If you love those who love you, what credit is that to you? For even sin-ners love those who love them ... love your enemies, do good, and lend, expecting nothing in return. Your reward will be great, and you will be children of the Most High; for he is kind to the ungrateful and the wicked. Be merciful (compas-sionate), just as your Father is merciful. (Luke 6:31-36)

Against the violent background of the arrest of Jesus, we get a glimpse of the tender compassion of Jesus. This is in sharp con-trast to the reaction of his disciples, a reaction which comes so easily to human nature, to meet violence with violence.

> When those who were around him saw what was coming, they asked, 'Lord, should we strike with the sword?' Then one of them struck the slave of the high priest and cut off his right ear. But Jesus said, 'No more of this!' And he touched his ear and healed him. (Lk 22:47-53)

FEATURE 6

The self-sacrificing spirit of Jesus

Generosity is a second feature which characterises the female side of affection. We have a lot of experience of this aspect of affection, for example, in the endless rounds parents go to provide their children with everything they need. They make great sacrifices to provide their children with the best education they can afford and they continue to do this even if their children show little appreciation of what is being done for them. I am often amazed at the generosity of my nephews and nieces towards their children and this brings home to me a heartfelt appreciation of all the trouble my parents went to so that I might have a good start in life and how they sacrificed so much for my sake.

Jesus shows his generosity by the amount of time and energy he devotes to caring for people. This feature of Jesus' love is foreshadowed in an image of God as our shepherd which the prophet Ezekiel was inspired to paint: a shepherd who spares no pains in looking after his sheep:

> I will feed them with good pasture, and the mountain heights of Israel shall be their pasture; there they shall lie down in good grazing land, and they shall feed on rich pasture on the mountains of Israel. I myself will be the shepherd of my sheep, and I will make them lie down, says the Lord God. I will seek the lost, and I will bring back the strayed, and I will bind up the injured, and I will strengthen the weak, but the fat and the strong I will destroy. I will feed them with justice. (Ezek 34:14-16)

Jesus uses this image of the good shepherd to reveal the full extent of his generosity as he describes the rounds he is willing to go to in establishing and maintaining the relationship he initiates with us. He is willing to spend himself leading us into his own relationship with his Father.

> He calls his own sheep by name and leads them out. When he has brought out all his own, he goes ahead of them, and the sheep follow him because they know his voice ... I am the good shepherd. I know my own and my own know me, just

as the Father knows me and I know the Father. And I lay down my life for the sheep. (Jn 10:1-15)

In the first three chapters of Mark's gospel we have a description of a typical day in the life of Jesus. We see how Jesus prepares people to listen to the good news by healing them of the wounds of the past and by setting them free from what enslaves them. In these three chapters Mark describes the concrete nature of Jesus' generosity in laying down his life for his sheep.

> That evening, after sunset, they brought to him all who were sick and those who were possessed by devils. The whole town came crowding around the door, and he cured many who were suffering from diseases of one kind or another; he also cast out many devils. (Mk 1:32-34)

Jesus' generosity can also be gauged from the profound nature of the gift he wants to share with us for it is a gift not just of all he has but of all that he is in self-disclosure. This gift is symbolised in the gospels by the feeding of the multitude where the references to Jesus taking the five loaves, looking up to heaven, blessing, and giving them to his disciples means that it is the Mass as the ultimate expression of Jesus' self-sacrificing generosity that is being referred to. 'And he did the same with the cup after supper, saying, This cup that is poured out for you is the new covenant in my blood.' (Lk 22:19-22)

A very striking characteristic of the generosity of Jesus is his capacity to continue to give himself to those who have proved themselves unfaithful to him. 'Simon, Simon, listen! Satan has demanded to sift all of you like wheat, but I have prayed for you that your own faith may not fail; and you, when once you have turned back, strengthen your brothers.' (Lk 22:31-34) Finally, he is very sensitive to the generosity of others.

> ... For all of them have contributed out of their abundance; but she out of her poverty has put in everything she had, all she had to live on. (Mk 12:41-44)

FEATURE 7

The extent and depth of Jesus' affection

The male dimension of affection seeks to expand the horizons of our affection. This growth is necessary if we are to receive and show affection within a wider world of relationships than we encounter within the home. So from an early age we are urged by our parents to develop friendships, to go to school and to become part of our local community. Thus we are called to constantly broaden our understanding of community as a circle of concern that surrounds us and to see how we might expand this circle of concern to include others. We are constantly invited to broaden the horizons of our affection even though this involves the difficult task of letting go of cherished ways of seeing and feeling about our world that we have outgrown.

In this feature we focus on the way that Jesus seeks to expand our horizons of his love for us. He does not want us to limit our capacity to receive his love and to return it. Rather he wants us to adopt the vision he puts before us of his all-encompassing love even though this involves a painful change of mind and heart. (Jn 12:24)

Whereas in the first half of each of the gospels Jesus makes himself known to his disciples as their Messiah, in the second half he reveals the kind of Messiah he is destined to be. The picture he paints for the disciples of the way he must travel as their Messiah is much more challenging than anything they had anticipated. They had expected him to be a triumphant Messiah who would liberate his people from Roman rule. However, the picture he paints of himself is of a messiah who will undergo great suffering, rejection and death. (Lk 9:22)

To help his disciples understand the price he is willing to pay to show the extent, depth and intensity of his affection, Jesus takes three of his disciples up the mountain of Tabor and there gives them a vision. In it they are invited to contemplate the broad canvas on which Jesus paints the whole picture of revelation, emphasising particularly the part his suffering and death have in the revelation of his love. (Lk 9:28-36)

Jesus challenges us to take the road he takes, sharing his sufferings and death on a daily basis. He invites us to die to ourselves by letting go of distorted ways of seeing ourselves so that we might accept the deep affection he has for us. This change of mind and heart is a real death but one that leads to new life.

> If any want to become my followers, let them deny themselves and take up their cross daily and follow me. For those who want to save their life will lose it, and those who lose their life for my sake will save it. What does it profit them if they gain the whole world, but lose or forfeit themselves? (Lk 9:23-25)

In the scene in Luke's gospel where Jesus joins two disciples on the road to Emmaus, we have another example of how he leads us to see our lives against the background of the story of his affection for us. We see the extent and depth of this affection in his sensitivity to and in his compassion for these two disciples. We see it too in the way he challenges them by means of the word of God to understand the meaning of his sufferings and of their own in the light of the love that is demonstrated in his death. However, it is above all in the 'breaking of bread' that they are challenged to face the full extent and depth of his affection for them. (Lk 24:13-35)

Jesus puts before us the means of maintaining the vision he reveals to us of how all-encompassing his affection is. He invites us to make space to listen, to savour and to assimilate the full extent and depth of his affection for us. 'Come away to a deserted place all by yourselves and rest a while.' (Mk 6:30-32) In that place apart Jesus invites us to pray as he did,

> In the morning, while it was still very dark, he got up and went out to a deserted place, and there he prayed. (Mk 1:35)

He also invites us to make time to participate in the Mass and thus to renew our vision of the depth of his love us.

> Those who eat my flesh and drink my blood abide in me, and I in them. (Jn 6:56)

FEATURE 8

An affection that involves Jesus' whole person

There is another way that the male dimension of affection challenges us to grow. This challenge is to develop the right balance
between four ways in which we show affection and receive it.
Even though we readily associate affection with physical and
emotional ways of manifesting it, there is also an intuitive and a
convictional level at which we can be affectionate. At an intuitive level we catch glimpses of one another which can be shared
if we take the pains to notice and express them. However, the
deepest and most enduring experience of affection consists in
the quiet growth, over a long period, of convictions about each
other's goodness and beauty. These convictions are often dormant but if they are given expression they can become the deepest
level at which we relate. One of life's tragedies is that these different levels of our affection fail to find expression for there is so
much to be gained if we become aware of and give expression to
the full range of our affection for others and become receptive to
theirs.

Jesus showed affection in the tactile way he related with those
he healed, touching the lepers even though the law forbade this.

> A leper came to him begging him, and kneeling he said to
> him, 'If you choose, you can make me clean.' Moved with
> pity, Jesus stretched out his hand and touched him, and said
> to him, 'I do choose. Be made clean!' (Mk 1:40-41)

Jesus gave expression to his feelings of deep affection for those
like the widow whose son he brought back to life. Luke says that
when he saw her 'his heart went out to her'. (Lk 7:13) Jesus is
also very insightful about the signs of affection he received from
the woman who anointed him and about her motivation in
doing so.

> But Jesus said, 'Let her alone; why do you trouble her? She
> has performed a good service for me ... she has anointed my
> body beforehand for its burial. Truly I tell you, wherever the
> good news is proclaimed in the whole world, what she has
> done will be told in remembrance of her.' (Mk 14:6-9)

It is hard to believe in the affection of others when we experience ourselves physically or emotionally at a distance from them. However, this sense of physical or emotional separation can also strengthen our convictions of their goodness and beauty if we make space for these to surface and be owned. The importance of these convictions is emphasised by Jesus when he invites Thomas to believe in his love for him even when Thomas has no sensate or felt experience of this love. It is this kind of affection that Thomas is invited to be open to when he declares that unless he can touch Jesus he will not believe.

> Have you believed because you have seen me? Blessed are those who have not seen and yet have come to believe. (Jn 20:24-29)

Even though faith is the ultimate experience of Jesus' affection we need to remain involved at the physical, emotional and intuitive levels as well. These four levels at which we receive and show affection are what the Great Commandment refers to when it invites us to be loved and to love with our whole 'heart, soul, mind and strength'. We are thus invited to get wholly and deeply involved in receiving and showing affection if we are to enter into life in the way that we are made to. (Lk 10:25-29) Jesus believes that the whole of revelation is about loving and being loved with our whole person within life's relationships.

> When the Pharisees heard that he had silenced the Sadducees, they gathered together, and one of them, a lawyer, asked him a question to test him. 'Teacher, which commandment in the law is the greatest?' He said to him, 'You shall love the Lord your God with all your heart, and with all your soul, and with all your mind.' This is the greatest and first commandment. And a second is like it: 'You shall love your neighbour as yourself.' On these two commandments hang all the law and the prophets. (Mt 22:34-40)

61

THE THIRD PORTRAIT

Provident love

We experience the provident love central to this portrait in people who are concerned for our welfare, especially that we would meet our deepest need in life which is to realise our dream. When people believe in us in this way and in all we are capable of becoming they give us *hope*. This gets us out on the road towards the realisation of our dream and sustains us on this journey. If our hope is to survive we need first of all to learn how to live constructively and contentedly with our *poverty*. This means that we must face our limitations in a realistic way and realise that we cannot reach the object of our hope on our own.

If we are to realise our dream we need *clarity of purpose*. This involves keeping in touch with our dream, constantly clarifying it and working out the most effective ways of realising it. We easily lose a sense of direction if we allow the demands of our more superficial dreams to deflect our sense of purpose. Clarity of purpose in turn invites us to work out the *practical implications* of realising our dream and of being true to ourselves.

Two of these practical needs that we must meet if we are to realise our dream are our need for freedom and for healing. We need *freedom* from being dominated by the preoccupations of our outer world if we are to have the time, energy and resources we need to devote to our inner one. If, due to a lack of space to meet the needs of our dream, we have become estranged from our true selves and from that of others, we are in need of the most radical kind of *healing*.

The features of the third portrait of Jesus

1. Jesus, whose main concern for us is that we realise our dream, loves us with a *provident love*. This concern is sensitive, pervasive and profound, covering all our needs both material and spiritual.

2. *Hope* defines the object of provident love as knowing the love of Jesus and the union and joy its magnetic power draws us into. Hope gets us out on the road towards this and sustains us on our way.

3. Christian hope is built on the *poverty of spirit* that is central to the Beatitudes. This is a spirit of dependence, trust and surrender that characterise the Christian response to the Father's provident love.

4. When Jesus says he is the *truth*, he further defines the object of our hope to be the love of his Father which he reveals in human terms. In fostering faith in this love, Jesus reveals the true self we dream of.

5. Seeing so clearly his Father's plan to make known his love gives Jesus great *clarity of purpose*. It is through keeping in touch with his Father's plan in prayer that Jesus remains focused on what is central.

6. Seeing the plan of the provident love of his Father so clearly, Jesus can focus on *the practical things that need to be done* to put this plan into action. He focuses especially on freeing people and healing them.

7. Jesus seeks *to set us free* from the distorted images of God, of ourselves and of others that block our belief in the good news of the Father's love and providence.

8. What Jesus seeks to heal is our sense of our insignificance which is a basic wound that we carry with us from the past. Jesus seeks to heal this wound by fostering faith in his good news.

FEATURE 1

Jesus' concern for all we may be

The love that distinguishes this feature is a provident one. It is a love we experience in the concern of people who want the best for us. We experience it as children in our parent's efforts to provide for us and it may only be when we have children of our own to provide for that we realise what an immense investment of time, energy and resourcefulness is involved in caring for children. Thus the love of concern that characterises this feature is shown in deeds more than in words, and it is distinguished by its extent and depth. This concern can be as extensive as looking after all the material needs of others and as profound as helping them to realise their dream.

This third portrait of Jesus centres on his provident love, one that is sensitive and deferential. He is sensitive to our material needs, to our feelings and to our unique gifts as well as to our deepest longings or dream. The deferential and considerate nature of Jesus' concern is seen in the way he relates with the woman he meets at a well in Samaria. He is so aware of where she is and of what she is ripe for, that he does not pressurise her to move on towards this but waits for her to respond to the various initiatives he takes. (Jn 4:1-42)

It is interesting to note how Jesus' concern for us is all-pervasive, covering all our needs, even our more material ones. At the marriage at Cana – prompted by the feminine sensitivity of Mary – Jesus works a miracle because of his concern to save the wedding party from the embarrassment of running out of wine.

> Jesus did this, the first of his signs, in Cana of Galilee, and revealed his glory; and his disciples believed in him. (Jn 2:11)

While Jesus' meeting with the woman at the well brings out the sensitivity and deference of his concern for us, the wedding at Cana brings out how pervasive or all-encompassing is this concern. (Jn 2:1-11)

This pervasive concern of Jesus for suffering humanity is the sign by which he is to be recognised as the one God sends to be our Messiah. When the disciples of John come to Jesus to find out if he is the Messiah, they are invited to judge for themselves on the basis of the very tangible signs of his concern which Jesus gives them.

> When John heard in prison what the Messiah was doing, he sent word by his disciples and said to him, 'Are you the one who is to come, or are we to wait for another?' Jesus answered them, 'Go and tell John what you hear and see: the blind receive their sight, the lame walk, the lepers are cleansed, the deaf hear, the dead are raised, and the poor have good news brought to them.' (Mt 11:2-5)

These signs or miracles which Jesus works in the gospels correspond to the wonderful works that God did for his people in the Exodus. The miracles like these wonderful works are a powerful source of revelation of Jesus' provident love for us.

The aim of Jesus' provident love for us is that we enjoy the life he comes to share with us. 'I came that they may have life, and have it abundantly.' (Jn 10:10) This life consists in coming to know Jesus' love which is that of his Father expressed in human terms. 'And this is eternal life, that they may know you, the only true God, and Jesus Christ whom you have sent.' (Jn 17:3) Making known his Father's love in this way is for Jesus his life's work.

> I made your name known to them, and I will make it known, so that the love with which you have loved me may be in them, and I in them. (Jn 17:26)

The climax of Jesus' life and his most profound act of provident love is his death and resurrection. It is belief in his and his Father's love, demonstrated by his death, that gives us a share in their 'eternal life'.

> And just as Moses lifted up the serpent in the wilderness, so must the Son of Man be lifted up, that whoever believes in him may have eternal life. For God so loved the world that he gave his only Son, so that everyone who believes in him may not perish but may have eternal life. (Jn 3:14-16)

FEATURE 2

A person full of hope

Deeply connected with the provident love of our family and friends, and the plans they have for us, is hope. This is a concern for, a reaching out towards all that might yet be in our lives. Hope is realistic in that it is sensitive to what we are ripe for, to what is now within our reach, for too much ambition has a deadening effect on us. When we clarify the object of our hope it gives us a sense of direction, gets us out on the road towards attaining it and encourages us not to give up.

In the Old Covenant what the people hoped for was symbolised by the Promised Land. This was seen as a place of plenty, 'a land flowing with milk and honey' largely because God would be with them in this place and on their journey there. This was the hope which inspired the Israelites to leave Egypt and to set out on their forty year journey across the desert. This hope sustained them on that journey in spite of all the difficulties they encountered. Then, through the prophets, the object of their hope became clearer.

> For surely I know the plans I have for you, says the Lord, plans for your welfare and not for harm, reserving a future full of hope for you. (Jer 29:11)

In this feature we will concentrate on the hope that Jesus in his provident concern sets before us. It is the hope of coming to know him and the full extent and depth of his love and so to enter into the life and happiness that results from this intimate knowledge. (Jn 17:3) Coming to know 'how wide and long and high and deep' Jesus' love is involves a life-long journey. This Exodus-like journey is depicted in the gospels as a journey to Jerusalem. In Luke's gospel especially, this journey which is central to his account of Jesus' life is seen as the new Exodus, with Jesus as the new Moses leading us to the new Promised Land. This symbolises the fullness of life that results from our sharing in Jesus' death and resurrection, from abiding in the love these events reveal.

Jesus said, 'The Son of Man must undergo great suffering,

and be rejected by the elders, chief priests, and scribes, and be killed, and on the third day be raised.' Then he said to them all, 'If any want to become my followers, let them deny themselves and take up their cross daily and follow me. For those who want to save their life will lose it, and those who lose their life for my sake will save it. What does it profit them if they gain the whole world, but lose or forfeit themselves? (Lk 9:22-25)

Immediately after this prediction Jesus shares a vision with his disciples. It is a vision which helps them to understand the meaning of all that is going to happen. In sharing this vision Jesus seeks to clarify the objective of his journey and of our hope.

Now about eight days after these sayings Jesus took with him Peter and John and James, and went up on the mountain to pray. And while he was praying, the appearance of his face changed, and his clothes became dazzling white. Suddenly they saw two men, Moses and Elijah, talking to him. They appeared in glory and were speaking of his departure [exodus], which he was about to accomplish at Jerusalem ... Then from the cloud came a voice that said, 'This is my Son, my Chosen; listen to him!' (Lk 9:28-36)

The prospect of knowing this love of Jesus for us, as the object of our hope, is what gets us out on the road to explore the extent and depth of his love and to make our own of it. His being 'lifted up' on the cross, which we remember at each Mass, 'draws' us with the magnetic power of its attractiveness to become aware of and to believe in Jesus' love. 'And I, when I am lifted up from the earth, will draw all people to myself.' (Jn 12:32) Just as the Promised Land was the symbol of hope for the people of the Old Covenant, the symbol of our hope is being with Jesus in the place he prepares for us.

I go to prepare a place for you, I will come again and will take you to myself, so that where I am, there you may be also. (Jn 14:3)

FEATURE 3

Jesus identifies with the poor

An essential part of our hope for the future is a sense of our human poverty that is rooted in our limitations and sinfulness. This kind of poverty inspires us to depend on the help of others rather than relying exclusively on our own resources. Life teaches us about our human poverty in that it asks us to admit that we cannot make it to the Promised Land on our own. Even though it is only common sense to face this shadow side of ourselves we may tend to repress it as something that belittles us. However, facing our poverty and living contentedly with it is realistic and healthy as it opens us up to the reality that we are not self-sufficient but need to rely on and trust in others on life's journey. If we do choose to face the less than ideal or shadow side of ourselves, we will learn how constructive this can be, that 'The shadow is 90% gold'. *(Carl Jung)*

As the tree's sap doth seek the root below
In winter, in my winter now I go
Where none but thee, the eternal root
Of true love, I may know.
(John Donne)

The attitude to life that Jesus taught in the Beatitudes is one of dependence, of trust and of surrender to God. It is an attitude that emerged during the exile in Babylon when the Israelites learned that to depend solely on their own resources to make something of themselves was mistaken. So they became 'the poor' when they learned that surrender to God's will or all-provident plan to make them a great people was a more realistic attitude to life. Jesus adopted this attitude of the poor as the key to the kingdom of God.

Happy are the poor in spirit, for theirs is the kingdom of heaven. (Mt 5:3)

Jesus often speaks of poverty of spirit in terms of our becoming a little child or one who is naturally dependent, trusting and called to obey his or her parents. Jesus sees this attitude of the child as the only realistic one to assume before God.

At that time the disciples came to Jesus and asked, 'Who is the greatest in the kingdom of heaven?' He called a child, whom he put among them, and said, 'Truly I tell you, unless you change and become like children, you will never enter the kingdom of heaven. Whoever becomes humble like this child is the greatest in the kingdom of heaven.' (Mt 18:1-4)

The poverty Jesus gives expression to in his life, and invites us to learn from him, rests on *a spirit of dependence on God* rather than on our own resources. (Mk 4:26-29) This attitude of poverty comes with the gradual realisation that we cannot achieve the object of our hope on our own but that we need to depend on others, and especially on the persons of the Trinity, without whom we 'can do nothing'; (Jn 15:5) it is 'only God who gives the growth.' (1 Cor 3:6-7)

Intimately related with dependence on God is *a spirit of trust.* It is based on the belief that the providence of God pervades the universe and that 'we can come to him with all our anxieties knowing that we are his personal concern.' (1 Pet 5:7) Jesus describes God's meticulous care even for the flowers of the field and invites us not to be anxious but to trust in how thorough his care is for us. (Lk 12:28-30) Prayer for Jesus is basically an expression of this trust. (Lk 11:11-13)

What makes poverty or humility the path to life is that its *child-like surrender* makes us receptive to what Jesus reveals to us. If we do not adopt this attitude we become, like the scribes and Pharisees, unreceptive to what Jesus wishes to reveal to us. (Mt 11:25-30) Jesus invites us to surrender to the slow, inconspicuous workings of God's providence.

> To what should I compare the kingdom of God? It is like yeast that a woman took and mixed in with three measures of flour until all of it was leavened. (Lk 13:20-21)

For Jesus, surrender to the will of his Father was his food or what gave him life. 'My food is to do the will of him who sent me and to complete his work.' (Jn 4:34)

FEATURE 4

'I am the truth'

In the first half of our lives we are involved in what is called our first journey. On it we seek to establish the outer circumstances that govern the way we want to live our lives; for example, we seek to establish ourselves in the work we do. As we enter the second half of life we are called to focus more of our attention and energies on our second journey. This is an inner journey on which nature calls us to focus more of our time and energies on answering our need to discover our true self and to share that self with others. This true self is in touch with our deepest longings or with our dream of relationships within which we are loved and seek to return this love. So we catch glimpses of our true selves in the eyes of those who accept and affirm us and it is our responsibility to capture and make our own of the truth they reflect back to us as in a mirror.

When Jesus speaks of himself as the truth he is not identifying with an intellectual truth such as that which we seek in the study of theology. The reason why Jesus identifies with the truth is because he expresses in his person the fullest revelation of God's love in human terms; (Jn 14:6-7) he is the embodiment of love living among us.

> And the Word became flesh and lived among us, and we have seen his glory, the glory as of a father's only son, full of grace and truth. (Jn 1:14) 'I am the way, and the truth, and the life. No one comes to the Father except through me. If you know me, you will know my Father also. From now on you do know him and have seen him.' Philip said to him, 'Lord, show us the Father, and we will be satisfied.' Jesus said to him, 'Have I been with you all this time, Philip, and you still do not know me? Whoever has seen me has seen the Father.' (Jn 14:6-9)

Jesus, as the truth, expresses God's love in human terms, or in a way that engages our whole person, our whole 'heart, soul, mind and strength'. Thus we get an intimate knowledge of what would otherwise be too intellectual or spiritual to engage our whole person. This is the way the Great Commandment directs us to relate and the way that Jesus recommends we immerse our whole selves in his love.

> You shall love the Lord your God with all your heart, and with all your soul, and with all your strength, and with all your mind; and your neighbour as yourself. (Lk 10:27) As the Father has loved me, so I have loved you; abide in my love. If you keep my commandments, you will abide in my love, just as I have kept my Father's commandments and abide in his love. (Jn 15:9-10)

In coming to know Jesus as the truth there is an invitation to accompany him on an inner journey on which we will discover, explore and assimilate the ultimate reality or truth in the 'breadth and length and height and depth' of his love.

> I pray that, Christ may dwell in your hearts through faith, as you are being rooted and grounded in love. I pray that you may have the power to comprehend, with all the saints, what is the breadth and length and height and depth, and to know the love of Christ that surpasses knowledge, so that you may be filled with all the fullness of God. (Eph 3:17-19)

The banquet at which Jesus wishes to satisfy our most fundamental hunger for the truth, or for God's love and all its attractiveness, is symbolised by the feeding of the multitude. (Jn 6:1-14) For John, the food at this banquet is 'the bread of life' a term which Jesus uses to indicate that he wishes to nourish us on life's journey both with his word and with his body and blood.

> Jesus said to them, 'I am the bread of life. Whoever comes to me will never be hungry, and whoever believes in me will never be thirsty.' (Jn 6:35) 'I am the living bread that came down from heaven. Whoever eats of this bread will live forever; and the bread that I will give for the life of the world is my flesh.' (Jn 6:51)

FEATURE 5

Jesus' clarity of purpose

As the provident love or the concern of those who love us deepens they want us to clarify our dream so that we may follow or realise it. This clarity of purpose is had through keeping in touch with and clarifying our dream and how we might realise it. However, if we are to attain this clarity of purpose, we will be faced with two options. The first is that we clarify our priorities so that we make our inner journey towards the realisation of our dream more and more central to life. The second is that we succumb to the temptation to remain on our outer journey towards more superficial dreams. If we allow ourselves to follow these, the object of our inner journey will remain clouded and we are likely to be seduced into giving centre stage to something other than to the relationships within which we find our true selves. For example, if we give the lion's share of our time, energy and resources to work we may have little left over for the intimate relationships that are meant to be the main concern of our second journey.

> It is not just as we take it
> This mystical world of ours;
> Life's field will yield as we make it
> A harvest of thorns or of flowers. *(Goethe)*

The story of the temptations of Jesus centres on three major forms of seduction which we easily yield to. They are in a general sense the temptations to pleasure, power and laziness and they are three ways we allow our clarity of purpose to be beclouded. What is remarkable in the way Jesus deals with these temptations is the clear and decisive way he names them for what they are and rejects them. The extent of Jesus' clarity and decisiveness is easily missed if we fail to realise that he 'was tempted in every way that we are', (Heb 4:15) or if we fail to acknowledge how subtle and pervasive these temptations are and how easily we succumb to them. (Lk 4:1-13)

With his clarity of purpose Jesus knows what needs to be done no matter what circumstances he finds himself in. He evaluates every situation in the light of his plan that we would come to know the Father's love as he does. As a means of keeping in touch with what he calls his Father's will he seeks the solitude needed to pray

> In the morning, while it was still very dark, he got up and went out to a deserted place, and there he prayed. And Simon and his companions hunted for him. When they found him, they said to him, 'Everyone is searching for you.' He answered, 'Let us go on to the neighbouring towns, so that I may proclaim the message there also; for that is what I came out to do.' (Mk 1:35-38)

Jesus reveals the secret of his clarity of purpose when he invites us to pray or to 'hear the word of God and do it'. Listening and responding to what Jesus reveals in the Mass and in his word is the main way he gives us of keeping in touch with and clarifying our purpose in life.

> Then his mother and his brothers came to him, but they could not reach him because of the crowd. And he was told, 'Your mother and your brothers are standing outside, wanting to see you.' But he said to them, 'My mother and my brothers are those who hear the word of God and do it.' (Lk 8:19-21)

We can see how Jesus draws his clarity of purpose from the word of God in the way he relates with his two disciples on the road to Emmaus. They have been thrown into confusion by the death of Jesus and are bent on escaping from what has become for them a sad and hopeless situation. Jesus helps them to understand what has happened with the help of the word of God and the Mass. As a result the two disciples regain their clarity of purpose and along with it a renewed sense of joy and enthusiasm.

> Were not our hearts burning within us while he was talking to us on the road, while he was opening the scriptures to us? That same hour they got up and returned to Jerusalem … Then they told what had happened on the road, and how they knew him in the breaking of the bread. (Lk 24:30-34)

FEATURE 6

The practical nature of Jesus' concern

Man alone of all the creatures of the earth can change his own pattern. Man alone is the architect of his own destiny. *(William James, The Principles of Psychology)*

Apart from human beings, the dream innate to everything in creation is automatically realised. If our dream is to be realised we have to become aware of it and then take responsibility for bringing it to be. Therefore, when we as human beings have become aware of and defined with some degree of clarity what is our dream we then need to devise the practical ways of realising it. After clarifying our priorities and how we plan to act on them, we need to translate these priorities and plans into action. Therefore, the people who make this feature real for us realise their ideals in a practical and efficient way.

Jesus is deeply involved in realising his ideals in a practical way. He lives out in his own life what he advocates in the gospels, which is that we need to 'act on' on the word of God as well as to listen to it. (Mt 7:24-29) The practical way Jesus does this astounds those who watch him.

> They were astounded beyond measure, saying, 'He has done everything well; he even makes the deaf to hear and the mute to speak.' (Mk 7:37)

In the parable of the good Samaritan, Jesus illustrates how he lives out in practice his ideal of loving others as we do ourselves. This practical nature of the love of the good Samaritan is what impresses the Scribe whose question prompts Jesus to tell the parable. When Jesus asks the Scribe to judge from the story who it is that shows himself a neighbour to the wounded man at the side of the road, he replies, 'The one who showed him practical sympathy.'

> But a Samaritan while travelling came near him; and when he saw him, he was moved with pity. He went to him and bandaged his wounds, having poured oil and wine on them. Then he put him on his own animal, brought him to an inn,

and took care of him. The next day he took out two denarii, gave them to the innkeeper, and said, 'Take care of him; and when I come back, I will repay you whatever more you spend.' (Lk 10:33-35)

The parable of the good shepherd also stresses the practical way Jesus realises his ideals. It is enlightening to ponder this parable in the context of the image of the shepherd in the prophet Ezekiel. There we have a portrait of God as our shepherd or gracious leader whose highly practical provident love guides, feeds, heals, looks after and gives rest to those who listen to his voice. (Ezek 34:11-16) The portrait of the good shepherd in John's gospel builds on this image as it focuses on the concrete way in which Jesus seeks to realise his sublime ideal that we should share the life he enjoys with his Father.

He calls his own sheep by name and leads them out. When he has brought out all his own, he goes ahead of them, and the sheep follow him because they know his voice … 'I came that they may have life, and have it abundantly. I am the good shepherd. The good shepherd lays down his life for the sheep.' (Jn 10:3-10)

Here we find Jesus calling us by name and guiding us into the pasture that his word and 'the bread of life' provides. This nourishment is the constant reminder, which the word and the Mass provide, that we are loved by the three persons of the Trinity in the unlimited way that they love each other. Jesus is willing to make any sacrifice, even that of his life, that we may believe or be convinced that we are loved in this passionate, permanent and personal way. (Jn 10:10-11)

It is to the realisation of this dream of making his Father known to us in a most profound and yet practical way that Jesus devotes his whole life.

I made your name known to them, and I will make it known, so that the love with which you have loved me may be in them, and I in them. (Jn 17:26)

It is to implement this plan that Jesus sends the Spirit to lead us into 'all the truth'. (Jn 16:13-15)

FEATURE 7

Jesus as one who set us free

We become aware of our lack of freedom when we find ourselves behaving, feeling or thinking in ways which we are not proud of. We may find ourselves behaving badly because we are prisoners of our feelings and of ways of seeing ourselves that give rise to these feelings. Well-established patterns of feeling and behaving make us feel that we are no longer free to be our true selves but that we are dominated by a bad spirit which disrupts our relationships with ourselves, with God and with others. However, people who love us and whose love we believe in have the power to set us free by helping us to change the way we see ourselves and thus how we feel.

> If I can be brought to realise, by the affirming and unconditional love of another, that I am really a decent and lovable person of considerable worth ... I will be gradually transformed into a self-confident, assured and happy person. *(John Powell, Fully Human Fully Alive)*

This feature is about a practical form of concern which Jesus spends a lot of time expressing in the gospels. It is his concern to set people free from being dominated by 'evil spirits' or from all that hinders their belief in the good news.

> The Spirit of the Lord is upon me, because he has anointed me to bring good news to the poor. He has sent me to proclaim release to the captives and recovery of sight to the blind, to let the oppressed go free, to proclaim a year of favour from the Lord. (Lk 4:18)

This practical concern of Jesus to liberate people from what oppresses them is demonstrated in his miracles. This is especially true of those miracles where he casts out the evil spirits that dominate our lives. In the first three chapters of Mark's gospel we have a description of a typical day in the life of Jesus. Very prominent is his work of liberating those who are possessed by 'unclean spirits'. (Mk 1:21-28)

In chapter five of his gospel Mark describes how a person called Legion is in the grip of an evil spirit. As a result he is forced to live in a graveyard apart from other people. The power and destructive nature of the spirits which possess him are emphasised in the failure of efforts to restrain him. When Jesus sets him free he sits at the feet of Jesus 'perfectly sane'. In other words, the man who was possessed by many evil spirits is now so enthralled by Jesus that he wants to be with him. To our surprise, Jesus asks him to remain with his own people and to tell them how kind Jesus has been to him. The story of Legion is all about how Jesus sets us free by enthralling us.

> They came to Jesus and saw the demoniac sitting there, clothed and in his right mind, the very man who had had the legion. (Mk 5:2-15)

What corresponds to the spirits called Legion within each of us (Mk 5:2-15) is the distorted images we have of ourselves and the destructive feelings that result from such images. If we are to be set free from this enslavement we need, like Mary, to sit at the feet of Jesus and listen to him. In this way we may learn to believe in his good news and in the light of this 'repent' or let go of those distorted images of ourselves which have enslaved us.

> Martha, Martha, you are worried and distracted by many things; there is need of only one thing. Mary has chosen the better part, which will not be taken away from her. (Lk 10:41-42)

It is above all by being 'lifted up' on the cross that Jesus manifests the love that sets us free. This love with all its powerful attractiveness draws us to him and thus enthralling us loosens the grip of what makes us unfree.

> You see, you can do nothing. Look, the world has gone after him! … And I, when I am lifted up from the earth, will draw all people to myself. (Jn 12:19, 32)

> Except you enthrall mee, never shall be free,
> Nor ever chast, except you ravish me. *(John Donne)*

FEATURE 8

Jesus' work of healing

The deepest wounds we can inflict on ourselves and the ones most in need of healing are those caused by the 'creeping separateness' that so easily effects our relationships. This separation can be due to what we do or fail to do when we disrupt or drift out of a relationship. The healing we need consists in being reconciled with ourselves and others and this involves getting in touch with and believing in those who by their acceptance and affirmation help us to accept and affirm ourselves.

In this feature we look at the healing work of Jesus which occupies such an important place in his ministry. A good context in which to understand his healing work is the parable of the good Samaritan. In it Jesus manifests that practical concern which does so much to heal the wounds we inflict on ourselves when we become separated from him.

The effects of this separation are described for us in the story of the Fall in chapters 1-12 of the book of Genesis. There we see what happens when people sin or separate themselves from God. They become estranged from themselves, from each other and from the whole of creation. Therefore, the most fundamental healing we are in need of is to be reconciled with God and thereby with ourselves and with others. In the parable of the vine and the branches Jesus sets before us the depth of the reconciliation and union he wants with us.

> I am the true vine, and my Father is the vinegrower. He removes every branch in me that bears no fruit. Every branch that bears fruit he prunes to make it bear more fruit ... Abide in me as I abide in you. Just as the branch cannot bear fruit by itself unless it abides in the vine, neither can you unless you abide in me. I am the vine, you are the branches. Those who abide in me and I in them bear much fruit, because apart from me you can do nothing. Whoever does not abide in me is thrown away like a branch and withers; such branches are gathered, thrown into the fire, and burned. (Jn 15:1-6)

After telling us this parable, Jesus gives us the recipe for this reconciliation. This is expressed in his commandment that we should love others as he loves us, that we should befriend all creation as he befriends us.

> This is my commandment, that you love one another as I have loved you. No one has greater love than this, to lay down one's life for one's friends. You are my friends if you do what I command you. I do not call you servants any longer, because the servant does not know what the master is doing; but I have called you friends, because I have made known to you everything that I have heard from my Father. (Jn 15:12-15)

The healing miracles in the gospels are faith-inducing signs of the provident love of Jesus. They are part of what Jesus terms 'the work of God' (Jn 6:29) and are thus akin to the wonderful works that God did for the Israelites in the Old Testament. Like those wonderful works, the miracles are signs which are meant to induce faith in the providence of God.

> My Father is still working, and I also am working. (Jn 5:17)

In healing two blind men Jesus seeks to elicit faith from them as it is this intimate knowledge of Jesus' concern for us that heals us at the deepest level. (Mt 9:27-31) For example, after healing the woman who suffered from a haemorrhage Jesus states explicitly that it is her faith, or her trust in his concern for her, which heals her. (Mk 5:34) Again, in the story of the cure of the paralytic the healing work of Jesus is associated with forgiveness. By our sins we separate ourselves from God and it is this which wounds us most seriously or paralyses us. It is Jesus' deep concern to forgive us our sins and so heal us at the deepest level by reconciling us to God again.

> And just then some people were carrying a paralysed man lying on a bed. When Jesus saw their faith, he said to the paralytic, 'Take heart, son; your sins are forgiven.' (Mt 9:1-8)

The personal love of Jesus

The people who make this portrait real for us love us in a personal way. They communicate *face to face* with the unique person in each of us and respect the fact that we are different and even unique. They highlight this by choosing us out of the crowd and, when they get to know us, they *call us by name* or address something unique to each of us.

There is a *perceptiveness* about the people who bring this portrait alive for us in that they tune in to the deeper meaning of what we say and do; they discern our thoughts, our feelings and what motivates us. As a result, these people identify easily with how we feel and we are aware that they know us intimately and can walk around with us in our experience. This capacity for *empathy* makes these people good listeners and they also have a capacity to *respond honestly* to what we say to them, at putting words on and sharing exactly how they feel. They are so perceptive and can empathise with deep feelings whether of joy or sorrow they are not thrown by strong feeling but can deal with them in a balanced way or with *equanimity*.

There is a distinctive style about the behaviour of the people who exemplify this portrait for us. They are sensitive and respectful in the way they *acknowledge* us and there is a style about what they say and what they do that finds expression in their *courtesy*. This for them is part of the supreme art, that of how we receive and return love within all our relationships.

The features of the fourth portrait of Jesus

1. Jesus expresses his *personal love* for us by relating with everybody one to one. Ultimately, he wants to draw us into the profoundly personal way he speaks face to face with his Father.

2. Jesus adds to the personal nature of the way he relates with us the reality that he not only chooses us out of the crowd but *calls us by name* into a relationship that is as unique for him as it is for us.

3. Jesus is highly *perceptive* in discerning how people think, feel and what motivates them to act. He is sensitive to the good that is in people as well as the good they are capable of.

4. Jesus is also highly responsive to what he senses is going on in us. He *empathises* with us in our weaknesses as well as with the wonder of our humanity and to the way his Father plans to glorify this.

5. Jesus is *emotionally honest* about this huge range of feeling he is capable of in his relationship with his Father and with us. He is equally forthright about his anger as he is about his joy.

6. Jesus' *equanimity* is revealed in the balanced way he holds together the extremes of feeling which he experiences in living with the agony and ecstasy of his own life and of the lives of those around him.

7. With all this sensitivity and responsiveness Jesus relates with all he meets in a most creative way. We see this in how he acknowledges the dignity, worth and glory of Zacchaeus, for example.

8. The artfulness with which Jesus relates is concretely expressed in the *courtesy* with which he treats his disciples. We see this after the resurrection when he prepares breakfast for them and serves it.

FEATURE 1

One who speaks with us face to face

People who give us an impression of this feature put us in touch with the world of relationships and with the importance of these in a world that is dominated for example by work. These people have a facility to relate with us as individuals, or face to face, rather than as part of a crowd. The personal quality of their relationships depends on what they share and on how they share this. So they relate in a personal way in the sense that they are willing to share something of their inmost selves and they invite those they relate with to do the same. Conversation at some depth is important for them as a way of engaging our whole person in our relationship with them. So they do not just share ideas but how they see and feel about their relationships.

The first feature of this portrait of Jesus focuses on the personal quality of the way he relates with people. In the gospel stories it is usually to individuals that he gives his attention more than to groups of people. A symbol of this way Jesus relates with individuals is given in the book of Exodus where we read that Moses 'spoke to God face to face, as one speaks to a friend'. (Ex 33:11)

In the Old Covenant God spoke to each person through Moses but in the New Covenant, as prophesised by Jeremiah, this personal or face to face relationship is extended to each person who is willing to enter it.

> The days are surely coming, says the Lord, when I will make a new covenant with the house of Israel and the house of Judah ... No longer shall they teach one another, or say to each other, 'Know the Lord,' for they shall all know me, from the least of them to the greatest, says the Lord. (Jer 31:31-34)

In the gospels Jesus fulfils this promise of a new covenant in the way that he relates with 'the least', in the form of outcasts and sinners, more than with those who like the scribes and Pharisees see themselves as 'the greatest'. Jesus seeks this intimately personal relationship with the weak and wayward person that is within each of us. (Mk 2:13-17)

Another aspect of the personal nature of the relationship Jesus wishes to establish with us is that he calls each of us to come to know him in the highly personal way that he knows his Father and his Father knows him. (Jn 10:14-15) He sees the setting up and the maintaining of this most personal relationship imaginable as his life's work.

> I made your name known to them, and I will make it known, so that the love with which you have loved me may be in them, and I in them. (Jn 17:26)

The personal way Jesus relates with us is part of the way the three persons of the Trinity are involved in making their love known to each person 'face to face' or personally. The Father sends Jesus to express this love in human terms and the Spirit leads us into an intimate knowledge of how 'wide and deep and long and high is the love of Christ'. (Eph 3:14-19, Jn 16:13-15)

Throughout the gospels Jesus is seen as initiating a conversation with each of us. In this conversation he wants us to listen to his self-disclosure and by responding honestly to disclose ourselves to him. This seems to be what Jesus has in mind when he invites us to listen and respond to his word as the key way of entering the deeply personal relationship he wants with us.

> 'Then pay attention to how you listen; for to those who have, more will be given; and from those who do not have, even what they seem to have will be taken away.' Then his mother and his brothers came to him, but they could not reach him because of the crowd. And he was told, 'Your mother and your brothers are standing outside, wanting to see you.' But he said to them, 'My mother and my brothers are those who hear the word of God and do it.' (Lk 8:18-21)

FEATURE 2

One who calls you by name

The experience of being chosen adds to the personal nature of a relationship. When we are chosen to do some work for someone we admire we feel honoured, as we experience a sense of being picked out of the crowd and of something distinctive about us being highlighted. Again, we might be chosen not just to do something but to be with the one who chooses us, to be a companion or a friend. As the person who chooses us comes to know us they may learn to call us by name or speak to the unique person they have come to know in us. Thus the relationship becomes increasingly personal as we share our unique selves.

The basis of the personal love we are looking at in this feature is the fact that we are each unique and that we want this uniqueness, or the dignity of our being different, to be recognised and respected. Each of us has a unique story and we can decide to share this unique thread of experience, this record of how our dream has unfolded. How personal a relationship is will depend both on what we share and on our method of sharing it. For example, when we relate in a personal way we often share something of ourselves and not just some information.

An important feature of the personal relationship Jesus seeks to establish with us is that he calls each of us by name. The influence of Jesus calling his disciples by name can be seen from their response to this personal call; very shortly after meeting him they leave everything to be with him.

> As he walked by the Sea of Galilee, he saw two brothers, Simon, who is called Peter, and Andrew his brother, casting a net into the sea – for they were fishermen. And he said to them, 'Follow me, and I will make you fish for people.' Immediately they left their nets and followed him. As he went from there, he saw two other brothers, James son of Zebedee and his brother John, in the boat with their father Zebedee, mending their nets, and he called them.

Immediately they left the boat and their father, and followed him. (Mt 4:18-22)

In his account of how Jesus calls the disciples, Mark focuses on the relationship with Jesus they are called to, as well as on what they are called to do. He describes how Jesus calls those whom he wants to be with him as companions into a very distinctive relationship with him.

He went up the mountain and called to him those whom he wanted, and they came to him. And he appointed twelve, whom he also named apostles, to be his companions and to be sent out to proclaim the message, and to have authority to cast out demons. (Mk 3:13-15)

In the first chapter of his gospel, John describes the nature of his own call and that of his companions with a series of very significant words. Jesus' invitation to 'Come and see' (Jn 1:39) means for John a call to come to know Jesus with all that the word 'know' means for him. Judging from the series of names John uses for Jesus there is a growing realisation of who he is for his disciples, and of who they are for him, in the intimate relationship he invites them into. (Jn 1:35-49) As we can see from the foregoing and from the way Jesus related with the man born blind, the distinctive relationship each of us has with Jesus does not remain static but changes as we come to know Jesus more intimately.

The man called Jesus ... He is a prophet ... If this man were not from God, he could do nothing ... Lord, I believe. And he worshipped him. (Jn 9:11, 17, 35-38)

In the parable of the good shepherd Jesus tells us that he calls each of us by our name.

'The gatekeeper opens the gate for him, and the sheep hear his voice. He calls his own sheep by name and leads them out. When he has brought out all his own, he goes ahead of them, and the sheep follow him because they know his voice.' (Jn 10:3-4)

FEATURE 3

Jesus perceives the good in everyone

It adds to the personal dimension of a relationship if those involved in it are perceptive about the mix of good and bad they find in each other. What is important in discerning this mix is that the basic dignity and goodness of people is the focus of interest. Therefore, if relationships are to grow, it is necessary to avoid what the book of wisdom calls 'the fascination of evil that obscures what is good'. (Wis 4:12) If people are perceptive about the good in each other and make it the context in which they accept their weakness then a personal relationship that is mainly positive, and yet realistic and honest, can grow.

We notice in the gospel story that Jesus is very sensitive to the good and bad influences at work on people. The Evangelists often note that Jesus knew what people were thinking or that he knew what was in their hearts.

> Even though he knew what they were thinking ... (Lk 6:8) But Jesus on his part would not entrust himself to them, because he knew all people and needed no one to testify about anyone; for he himself knew what was in everyone. (Jn 2:24-25)

This capacity of Jesus to discern what is going on in people is very striking in a world that is often unaware of the forces influencing it and also where it is being led by these forces. This perceptiveness of Jesus is seen in the way he invites us to take responsibility for the influences at work in us and for where these are leading us. He would have us face this dark side of our lives that leads to 'destruction' as well as the bulk of our experience that leads to 'life'.

> 'Enter through the narrow gate; for the gate is wide and the road is easy that leads to destruction, and there are many who take it. For the gate is narrow and the road is hard that leads to life, and there are few who find it.' (Mt 7:13-14)

There is a striking scene in Matthew's gospel which reveals how keenly aware Jesus is of how the bad spirit leads us down the 'road to destruction'. In the scene Jesus reveals how astute he is in his observations about the malicious spirit at work in those who accused him of being in league with the devil. He observes that their prejudice does not allow them to see that in working miracles he is overcoming the influence of the devil. He also perceives how their prejudice, generated by hatred, causes a wilful blindness that cuts them off from God's influence.

He knew what they were thinking and said to them, 'Every kingdom divided against itself is laid waste, and no city or house divided against itself will stand. If Satan casts out Satan, he is divided against himself; how then will his kingdom stand?' (Mt 12:25-37)

Jesus is highly perceptive in the way he discerns the workings of the good spirit in people. For example, he judges with great astuteness the time and the way to call Peter (Lk 5:1-11). He also grasps the precise moment when Peter is ready to let his betrayal of him be turned into a humbler and deeper love, a love that eventually involves giving his life for Jesus. (Jn 21:15-18)

Jesus detects the seeds of greatness in Zacchaeus, in the Samaritan woman and in the woman in Simon's house, and he judges with great acumen how to lead them to belief in him and in themselves. He has a discerning eye for the seeds of greatness even though these may seem so small and insignificant in their beginnings. 'With what can we compare the kingdom of God, or what parable will we use for it? It is like a mustard seed, which, when sown upon the ground, is the smallest of all the seeds on earth; yet when it is sown it grows up and becomes the greatest of all shrubs.' (Mk 4:31-32) Jesus perceives the goodness in people in the most ordinary circumstances and he seeks to highlight this.

Truly I tell you, this poor widow has put in more than all those who are contributing to the treasury. For all of them have contributed out of their abundance; but she out of her poverty has put in everything she had. (Mk 12:41-44)

FEATURE 4

Jesus' capacity for empathy

The saying of the French writer Blaise Pascal that 'The heart has reasons of which the reason knows nothing' highlights the truth that there is an intimate knowledge of others that arises when we feel so deeply for them that we empathise with them. This capacity for empathy adds an important dimension to the personal quality of our relationships. It is a rare enough dimension for it demands that we are in touch with our own suffering as it is our experience of this that gives us the ability to enter into the sufferings of others.

> Unto a broken heart no other one may go without the high prerogative itself hath suffered too. *(Emily Dickenson)*

In this feature we will look at the sensitive way Jesus relates with people and more specifically at his capacity for empathy. Jesus has the power to feel for others, to identify with them and thus fully comprehend them. He is a revelation of the empathy of God who knows us through and through.

> Yahweh, you examine me and know me, you know if I am standing or sitting, you read my thoughts from far away, whether I walk or lie down, you are watching, you know every detail of my conduct ... Such knowledge is beyond my understanding, a height to which my mind cannot attain ... You know me through and through. (Ps 139:1-6, 15)

The foundation of Jesus' capacity for empathy is laid in his incarnation. As a result, he identifies with our humanity, its strengths and weaknesses, its joys and sorrows. In assuming the role of the Suffering Servant, which he does at his baptism, Jesus shoulders not only his own weakness but the consequences of the weakness and sinfulness of humanity. (Heb 4:15) Again, by washing the feet of his disciples Jesus gives us a powerful symbol of his wish to identify with our humanity by being with us as 'one who serves'. (Lk 22:27, Jn 13:13-17)

Jesus sees himself as part of the *anawim* or of those who live out of the Beatitudes in total dependence on and complete surrender to God. He identifies with this essential condition of being human and limited and invites us to learn this attitude from him.

> Take my yoke upon you, and learn from me; for I am gentle and humble in heart, and you will find rest for your souls. (Mt 11:29)

Because Jesus becomes 'like us in every respect' he can empathise with us in everything. He is familiar with all our weakness and 'in every respect has been tested as we are'. (Heb 2:16-18)

> For we do not have a high priest who is unable to sympathise with our weaknesses, but we have one who in every respect has been tested as we are, yet without sin. (Heb 4:15)

We see how deeply Jesus identifies with us in our sufferings as, for example, he identifies with the sufferings of Martha and Mary at the death of their brother; (Jn 11:33-40) he has the rare ability to enter the sufferings of others even when he is immersed in his own. (Lk 23:26-32) When Jesus weeps over Jerusalem he shows how deeply he feels the tragedy of his own people's failure to recognise 'the things that make for peace'.

> As he came near and saw the city, he wept over it, saying, 'If you, even you, had only recognised on this day the things that make for peace! But now they are hidden from your eyes.' (Lk 19:41-44)

Jesus' empathy, or his power to understand and imaginatively enter our world of positive feelings, is seen in his farewell address to his disciples when he speaks about his lifelong desire to share with them the relationship he has with his Father, to share the glory and the love they enjoy. (Jn 17:21-23) From the beginning of his life to its end Jesus wishes to share not only his cross but above all his resurrection and all the feelings of joy and enthusiasm that are part of it. (Lk 2:8-11) Even though his disciples are sad when the time comes for him to ascend to his Father, it is their faith and hope in Jesus' love, and the joy these give rise to, that prevails. (Lk 24:50-52)

FEATURE 5

The emotional honesty of Jesus

Our feelings have an important role to play in the way we relate with others. If our emotional life has been neglected, it may be because we are not convinced that our feelings have an important role to play in the way we relate. As a result of this low estimation we have of our feelings we may have difficulty giving time to noticing and expressing them. However, if we do become good at expressing our feelings, we will find that they have a huge contribution to make towards the personal quality of our relationships.

Being emotionally honest is for Jesus an important element in expressing the intimate relationship he has with his Father and that he now wants to draw us into. All through his life Jesus seeks with a passion to make himself known to us and to reveal the love he feels for us as well as all the feelings of joy and enthusiasm that surround this love. In chapters 14-17 of John's gospel Jesus speaks with great feeling as he invites us to celebrate the love, the glory, the intimacy and the joy he wants to share with us. (Jn 14:15-26, 15:9-15, 16:12-15, 25-33, 17:20-26)

> The glory that you have given me I have given them, so that they may be one, as we are one, I in them and you in me, that they may become completely one, so that the world may know that you have sent me and have loved them even as you have loved me. Father, I desire that those also, whom you have given me, may be with me where I am, to see my glory, which you have given me because you loved me before the foundation of the world. Righteous Father, the world does not know you, but I know you; and these know that you have sent me. I made your name known to them, and I will make it known, so that the love with which you have loved me may be in them, and I in them. (Jn 17:22-26)

Jesus is emotionally open about what makes him feel sorrowful and frustrated. For example, he voices in very strong terms his disappointment with the way that many people do not respond to his call to conversion. (Mt 11:20-24) He is very explicit too in his response to his hour of heartbreak in Gethsemane where he reveals how vulnerable the prospect of his sufferings makes him feel.

> Jesus began to be distressed and agitated. And said to them, 'I am deeply grieved, even to death; remain here, and keep awake.' And going a little farther, he threw himself on the ground and prayed that, if it were possible, the hour might pass from him. He said, 'Abba, Father, for you all things are possible; remove this cup from me; yet, not what I want, but what you want.' (Mk 14:32-42)

During the hours of darkness of his passion and death Jesus gives full expression to the depth of his sense of abandonment. (Mk 15:33-34) He also expresses his confidence in the one to whom he has committed himself. (Lk 23:46) He shows his emotional honesty in the way that he assertively confronts infidelity, hypocrisy and injustice. We see this in the way he confronts Peter about his denial (Lk 22:31-34), Judas about his betrayal (Lk 22:21-23) and the scribes and Pharisees about their greed, hypocrisy and injustice. (Mt 23:25-28)

It is striking how forthright Jesus is in his appreciation and praise of people like the woman in Simon's house. (Lk 7:36-50) Similarly, he does not let the significance of the simple gesture of a woman's anointing him go unacknowledged even though those around him reject the woman's gesture as excessive.

> Truly I tell you, wherever the good news is proclaimed in the whole world, what she has done will be told in remembrance of her. (Mk 14:9)

Again, Jesus expresses his feelings of deep appreciation of the centurion's faith. (Lk 7:9) Even though Jesus is well aware of how fragile his disciples are and how they will desert, deny and betray him, this does not prevent him from showing how much he appreciates their loyalty to him. (Mt 19:28) He also expresses his passionate concern that his disciples would be able to enter fully into life's sorrows and find the peace that is part of doing this. (Jn 16:21-22)

FEATURE 6

Jesus faces life's joys and sorrows with equanimity

With today's exaggerated interest in the darker side of human nature there is a need for a better balance between this and all that is positive. From a more healthy balance of the light and darkness of life springs equanimity. This is an evenness of feeling that avoids the wild, emotional swings caused especially by misfortune. It faces life's peaks and valleys, its joys and sorrows not by repressing them in a stoical way but by giving them expression in a passionate and yet measured way.

Jesus lives at ease with the reality that he is the divine word become human and ordinary. (Jn 1:14) He so combines the extremes of the divine and the human that the ordinary becomes extraordinary and the extraordinary becomes ordinary. Jesus walks with both these extremes in a calm, balanced way and invites us to do the same. (Lk 9:28-36)

Jesus begins his public life with a manifestation of his equanimity in response to the dramatic event of his baptism. By insisting that John baptise him with his baptism of repentance, Jesus enters fully into the dark world of our sinfulness. How fully he does this is described in the letter to the Hebrews where it says that he is 'familiar with all our weakness and was tempted in every way that we are, but without sin.' (Heb 4:15) This immersion of Jesus, not just in our human condition but in all the consequences of our sinfulness, is portrayed for us in the temptation in the desert which follows immediately on his baptism. (Mt 4:1-11) At the same time Jesus is conscious of himself as God's 'beloved', as the one in whom God delights.

> Then Jesus came from Galilee to John at the Jordan, to be baptised by him. John would have prevented him, saying, 'I need to be baptised by you, and do you come to me?' But Jesus answered him, 'Let it be so now; for it is proper for us in this way to fulfil all righteousness.' Then he consented. And when Jesus had been baptised, just as he came up from the water, suddenly the heavens were opened to him and he saw the Spirit of God descending like a dove and alighting on

him. And a voice from heaven said, 'This is my Son, the Beloved, with whom I am well pleased.' (Mt 3:13-17)

We find a striking manifestation of the equanimity of Jesus in the way he deals with the agony and the ecstasy associated with the prospect of his passion, death and resurrection. He tells us about the extremes of sorrow and joy which these events cause him in chapters 14-17 of John's gospel. Jesus sees his life as a journey towards his death and resurrection and during his public life he speaks of these most dramatic events of his life in a passionate and yet calm way.

They were on the road, going up to Jerusalem, and Jesus was walking ahead of them; they were amazed, and those who followed were afraid. He took the twelve aside again and began to tell them what was to happen to him, saying, 'See, we are going up to Jerusalem, and the Son of Man will be handed over to the chief priests and the scribes, and they will condemn him to death; then they will hand him over to the Gentiles; they will mock him, and spit upon him, and flog him, and kill him; and after three days he will rise again.' (Mk 10:32-34)

We see the equanimity of Jesus especially in his resurrection when he enters his glory. We find this in the charming, low-key way he appears to his disciples in the lakeside scene described in John's gospel. There we find him displaying what John terms his 'glory' by being familiar and gracious to those who had betrayed and deserted him in his hour of need. (Jn 21:1-17) Jesus has the facility to live contentedly with the mixture of good and bad, the light and darkness, the weeds and wheat of each person's life. (Mt 13:24-30) In his parable of the weeds amid the wheat Jesus challenges us to live as contentedly as he does with the weeds amid the wheat in our own lives and in the lives of those around us. Jesus wants us to face life and death, joy and sorrow with the same healthy balance of feeling, with the same mixture of passion and contentment as he did.

FEATURE 7

Jesus acknowledges everyone as significant

To acknowledge people as significant for us involves paying attention to them as well as respecting them. In effect, it involves saying to people, 'It is good that you are.' Each of us has the experience of walking into a crowded room and not being noticed by some people but being recognised and made to feel significant by others. We remember with affection those people who when we were young acknowledged us in the sense that they had a word for us when we met them, made a fuss of us, treated us as important.

The capacity of Jesus to acknowledge everyone as important and significant for him is an essential part of the new covenant he comes to set up. This covenant, announced by the prophet Jeremiah, is all about God's self-revelation, not to the chosen few but to the least no less than to the greatest. (Jer 31:33-34)

In the story of Zacchaeus we notice this ability of Jesus to acknowledge people. We see how he makes Zacchaeus the centre of attention where at the beginning of the scene he is out on the periphery of the crowd. Those standing around Zacchaeus do not approve of what Jesus is doing as they would like to exclude Zacchaeus from the community because he is a tax collector. Jesus, however, challenges their estimation of Zacchaeus by highlighting his dignity. He highlights the fact that Zacchaeus is just as much a son of Abraham as any of them and one with whom he wishes to enjoy table fellowship.

> When Jesus came to the place, he looked up and said to him, 'Zacchaeus, hurry and come down; for I must stay at your house today.' So he hurried down and was happy to welcome him. All who saw it began to grumble and said, 'He has gone to be the guest of one who is a sinner' .... 'he too is a son of Abraham. For the Son of Man came to seek out and to save the lost.' (Lk 19:5-10)

In Jesus' time children had little or no status but Jesus insists on acknowledging their importance for him by making time for them in his busy day. He is angry with those who would deny their right to his attention and the way he takes them in his arms is a striking sign of their importance for him.

> People were bringing little children to him in order that he might touch them; and the disciples spoke sternly to them. But when Jesus saw this, he was indignant and said to them, 'Let the little children come to me; do not stop them; for it is to such as these that the kingdom of God belongs. Truly I tell you, whoever does not receive the kingdom of God as a little child will never enter it.' And he took them up in his arms, laid his hands on them, and blessed them. (Mk 10:13-16)

Even though those who are sick and disabled are often neglected by society, Jesus acknowledges their importance for him. He always finds time for them and makes them the centre of attention even if he thus incurs the wrath of the powers that be and even endangers his own life. (Mk 3:1-6) Jesus acknowledges how important sinners and outcasts are for him and he insists that they possess virtues that the so-called virtuous often lack. (Lk 18:8-14)

In the parable of the good Samaritan Jesus declares that his respect has no boundaries. In this parable it is striking that the Samaritan differs in race and creed from the badly injured Jew on the side of the road. (Lk 10:31-33) Jesus gives an example of one of the many ways he is the good Samaritan when he is approached by a leper. Jesus does not hesitate to help him even though he is forbidden to do so by the law.

> Moved with pity, Jesus stretched out his hand and touched him, and said to him, I do choose. Be made clean! (Mk 1: 40-41)

Jesus is conscious of the dignity of everybody he meets, such as the Roman centurion, (Mk 1:40-41, Mt 8:10) and seeks to raise their consciousness of this in the light of the overwhelming truth that each person is loved by Jesus and the Father just as they love each other.

> You have loved them even as you have loved me. (Jn 17:23)

FEATURE 8

The courtesy Jesus shows to one and all

We might think of courtesy in a number of ways. We might see it as what is expected of us in different situations or as a formal way of behaving that we need to adhere to if we wish to be accepted in society. Again, we might see courtesy as an expression of our respect for human dignity, as a certain way of behaving that is in keeping with that dignity. Finally, we might see courtesy in a Christian context, or as part of the greatest of all the arts, the art of loving.

> Of Courtesy, it is much less
> Than Courage of Heart or Holiness,
> Yet in my walks it seems to me
> That the Grace of God is in Courtesy.
> *(Hilaire Belloc)*

In the following quotation from Luke's gospel, Jesus portrays himself as the one who reveals what he calls God's 'gracious will'. In Jesus this 'gracious will' becomes incarnate and is embodied in the gracious words he speaks and in the courteous way he relates.

> At that same hour Jesus rejoiced in the Holy Spirit and said, 'I thank you, Father, Lord of heaven and earth, because you have hidden these things from the wise and the intelligent and have revealed them to infants; yes, Father, for such was your gracious will.' (Lk 10:21)

The word *gracious* means kind, considerate, polite or courteous and even though we may associate a word like courtesy with refined manners or social graces, it has its roots in love or in its 'courtesy of the heart'. 'There is a courtesy of the heart. It is akin to love. Out of it arises the purest courtesy in our outward behaviour.' (*Goethe*) When applied to Jesus the word *courtesy* emphasises the practical expression of the graciousness of God which Jesus makes tangible. The personal way that Jesus relates with people is characterised by a great sensitivity towards everyone. As well as being sensitive, Jesus also responds to people in a respectful way. These attitudes form the courtesy of the heart that finds expression in Jesus' actions. (Jn 1:18)

In his book *The Art of Loving*, Erich Fromm makes the point that the greatest of all the arts, and perhaps the most undervalued, is that of loving. Since Jesus is the revelation of God's love in human terms, it follows that he has developed this art to a high degree in the way he speaks and acts. There is a refined style that characterises the way he relates with each person he meets. Certainly this was the impression of those who listened to him. Luke tells us that they

> All spoke well of him and were amazed at the gracious words that came from his mouth. They said, 'Is not this Joseph's son?' (Lk 4:22)

In describing the gracious way the father receives his prodigal son in chapter 15 of Luke's gospel, Jesus is describing the courtesy of God. We can see how this divine courtesy is revealed in Jesus' life in the way he deals with people like the woman in Simon's house. We see how he graciously acknowledges how significant is her gesture of washing his feet with her tears and of drying them with her hair. Jesus does not share in the deep embarrassment of his fellow guests and reject her as they wanted him to do. Instead, he shows his respect for her and for the great love that motivates what she does for him.

> You gave me no water for my feet, but she has bathed my feet with her tears and dried them with her hair. (Lk 7:44-47)

It is in the really testing circumstances of the betrayal of Judas that we see the true quality of the courtesy of Jesus. (Mt 26:20-25, 47-50) We see it too in Jesus' consideration for the feelings of his disciples when he meets them after they have deserted him when he needed them most. (Jn 21:1-14) It is very striking how Jesus takes the initiative in reconciling them with himself by preparing breakfast for them and by serving it. 'When they had gone ashore, they saw a charcoal fire there, with fish on it, and bread. And Jesus said to them, Come and have breakfast!' (Jn 21:15-19)

The profound love of Jesus

This portrait focuses on our experience of being loved deeply or profoundly and on the specific kind of *wisdom* being loved in this way give us. This wisdom can range from having an overall vision of life that gives it meaning and direction to that interior knowledge we get from our experience of getting our whole person involved in *being loved* and in being loving within the main relationships of life.

To avoid making our experience of wisdom too abstract or too spiritual we need to think of it *in human terms* or as coming to us through our senses, feelings, images and convictions as much as through our minds. In other words, wisdom comes to us in the ordinary way we know those people who love us and whom we love. This wisdom which is primarily the fruit of our personal experience is expanded, clarified and deepened if we draw on the more universal experience that is available to us in the *traditional wisdom* of the community. This wisdom is mediated to us through stories, poems and proverbs.

The wisdom figures in our lives *generously* share the wisdom they have gleamed from their own experience and which they have reflected on in the light of traditional wisdom. They *communicate* this wisdom mainly through conversation in which they share in depth. They *communicate assertively* by drawing us out, listening attentively to what we have to say and by responding honestly and positively to this. To maintain this conversation and the relationships it establishes, they challenge us to make space for reflection and for sharing its fruits. Finally, the wisdom figures in our lives are good at *delegating*. They do not want us to be permanently dependent on them for our wisdom but invite us to become aware of and to trust in our own.

The features of the fifth portrait of Jesus

1. *The profound nature of Jesus' love* or *his wisdom* is based on the intimate knowledge he has of his Father's love. This provides him with an all-inclusive vision that gives everything its true meaning and value.

2. *At the core of Jesus' wisdom* is his interior knowledge of being loved and of loving his Father. Since they love us as they do each other, we can glimpse Jesus' wisdom in our experience of their love.

3, In becoming a human being, Jesus reveals a vision of his Father's love *in human terms* so that their wisdom becomes real for us as it is addressed to our whole person 'heart, soul, mind and senses'.

4. In his word and in the Mass, Jesus provides us with *a context in which we can understand* our personal experience; we see the wisdom of our own story within that which the Bible, and especially the gospel, tells.

5. *Generosity* is a feature of Jesus' wisdom seen in the way he shares everything he has and is with us. He uses images of the banquet, the feeding of the multitude and the Mass to highlight this.

6. The depth of Jesus' love or his wisdom is offered to us through a *conversation* Jesus initiates when he reveals himself to us. By listening and responding to Jesus we learn who he is for us and we for him.

7. Jesus *challenges us assertively* to make space to listen and respond to his word as our relationship with him depends heavily on the quality of this communication.

8. Jesus *delegates his life's work* to us, leaving us free to do it as we think best. He trusts us with what is extremely precious to him and remains profoundly supportive even when we abuse his trust.

FEATURE 1

A wisdom born of being loved

People may be considered wise on a number of grounds. It may be because they are knowledgeable on a particular topic, or because of their intellectual mastery of some branch of knowledge. Sometimes wisdom is judged on the basis of a person's acumen in handling their monetary affairs. Again wisdom may be seen in terms of good judgement in handling one's personal relationships, or it may be an interior knowledge we get when we love another wholly and deeply or when another loves us in this way.

When we speak of the profound love of Jesus and identify it with his wisdom, we are dealing with a knowledge that emerged in the wisdom literature of the Bible. There wisdom is identified with an intimate knowledge that has its source in the experience of being loved and of being loving. It is this intimate knowledge or wisdom that Jesus talks about when he says that he knows us and we can know him, just as the Father knows him and he knows the Father.

> I am the good shepherd. I know my own and my own know me, just as the Father knows me and I know the Father. And I lay down my life for the sheep. (Jn 10:14-15)

Wisdom can be seen as an all-inclusive vision. For Jesus this vision gives our lives meaning and direction for it provides us with a healthy overview that allows us to see everything in perspective. (Mt 5:13-16) This all-inclusive vision which Jesus puts before us centres on his revelation of his Father's love. In the sense that Jesus embodies this revelation, he *is* this wisdom and not only proclaims it.

> Have I been with you all this time, Philip, and you still do not know me? Whoever has seen me has seen the Father. How can you say, 'Show us the Father?' Do you not believe that I am in the Father and the Father is in me? (Jn 14:6-11)

There is a view of wisdom, common throughout the wisdom books of the Bible, as what enables us to discern which ways of behaving are consistent with our basic vision and which are not. This ability to discern gives us an intimate knowledge of how to speak and act, especially when we are dealing with difficult situations. Jesus expresses this kind of wisdom, for example, in his parable of the two ways. (Mt 7:13-14)

The all-inclusive vision of Jesus centres on what is at the heart of his wisdom. This is an intimate knowledge of being loved by and of loving his Father. So a further understanding of Jesus' wisdom comes from his experience of loving the Father and us. Love makes us wide-eyed or perceptive about the goodness of those we love deeply. Because he loves his Father so deeply, he has a unique perception of his Father which he wants to reveal to us.

No one has ever seen God. It is God the only Son, who is close to the Father's heart, who has made him known. (Jn 1:18)

Because Jesus loves us so deeply he has an extraordinary perception of all that makes us so lovable for him. He perceives a depth of goodness in the woman in Simon's house that he is intent on revealing to her and to Simon, in spite of his reluctance to accept it. (Lk 7:39-40, 47-50)

A final way of understanding the wisdom of Jesus is the most basic one. It consists in an intimate knowledge he has of being loved by his Father. Knowing that he is loved in this way, and the intimacy and happiness which springs from this, dominates John's picture of Jesus and especially that which we find in chapters 14-17 of his gospel.

As the Father has loved me, so I have loved you; abide in my love. If you keep my commandments, you will abide in my love, just as I have kept my Father's commandments and abide in his love. I have said these things to you so that my joy may be in you, and that your joy may be complete. (Jn 15:9-11) I made your name known to them, and I will make it known, so that the love with which you have loved me may be in them, and I in them. (Jn 17:23-26)

FEATURE 2

The core of Jesus' wisdom

In this feature we focus on a view of profound love or wisdom that centres on the basic relationships of our lives and on the intimate knowledge we get of being loved and loving within these relationships. Each of us has to ask ourselves how real it is for us to put our relationships at the heart of our wisdom and to put love at the heart of these relationships. If it does not seem realistic to do this, then the wisdom of Jesus which we find in the gospels will not talk to our experience. As a result it will appear unreal and not engage us.

We are told by Luke that Jesus grew in wisdom with the years and that he learned it on a journey that began in Nazareth and took him to his death out of love for us in Jerusalem. 'And as the child grew to maturity, he was filled with wisdom.' (Lk 2:40) This kind of wisdom is mysterious but we can get some understanding of it from the words that are used to describe Jesus' relationship with his Father. We have seen already that at the heart of Jesus' wisdom is an intimate knowledge that he had of being loved by his Father and of returning that love. When he leaves his home in Nazareth and arrives at the Jordan river to be baptised by John the Baptist, he hears himself addressed as his Father's 'Beloved'. This image of Jesus as the beloved is often used whenever the Father addresses Jesus in the gospels.

> This is my Son, the Beloved, with whom I am well pleased.
> (Mt 3:17)

This image of himself as the beloved would have been familiar to Jesus from the servant songs in the prophet Isaiah. The growing consciousness of being the beloved in whom his Father delights gradually shapes the wisdom of Jesus, his consciousness of how profound was the love of his Father for him. 'Here is my servant, whom I uphold, my chosen, in whom my soul delights; I have put my spirit upon him.' (Is 42:1-2)

The term which John uses at the beginning of his gospel for Jesus, when he calls him the 'Word', is very close in meaning to the term wisdom. By calling Jesus the word John means that

Jesus is the revelation in human terms of the love of his Father. Since he is 'full of grace and truth' or a revelation of the loving-kind and faithful love of God, he must have had an intimate knowledge of this love which he was sent to reveal to us.

> And the Word became flesh and lived among us, and we have seen his glory, the glory as of a father's only son, full of grace and truth. (Jn 1:14)

Another word that John often uses to express Jesus' relationship with his Father is also used to express the wisdom of Jesus. This is the word 'know' and when it is used by Jesus in a phrase like 'I know the Father and the Father knows me' it means that they have an interior knowledge of being loved by each other. It is in this interior knowledge of being wholly and deeply loved that the wisdom of Jesus consists.

> I know my own and my own know me, just as the Father knows me and I know the Father. (Jn 10:14-15)

The intimate knowledge of being the Father's beloved which forms the wisdom of Jesus is a mysterious knowledge. We get glimpses of what it is like from what Jesus says about the way they know and love each other. However, since Jesus and the Father love us just as they love each other we get a more concrete and intimate knowledge of their love for each other from our experience of the way they love us. (Jn 15:9-15, 14:15-24)

> I know my own and my own know me, just as the Father knows me and I know the Father. And I lay down my life for the sheep. (Jn 10:14-15) ... As the Father has loved me, so I have loved you; abide in my love. (Jn 15:9) The glory that you have given me I have given them, so that they may be one, as we are one, I in them and you in me, that they may become completely one, so that the world may know that you have sent me and have loved them even as you have loved me. (Jn 17:22-23)

FEATURE 3

A wisdom expressed in human terms

Our ideas about wisdom can be largely intellectual and remote from our daily experience. If this happens, our personal experience, based on our senses, feelings and intuitions, may not be seen as having much value and as not having much to contribute to our notion of wisdom. However, if we accept that *wisdom is an interior knowledge of being loved and of returning this love* then much of this wisdom will come from the four ways we are loved and return that love, which is through our senses, feelings, intuitions and convictions. Therefore the wisdom we are looking at in this feature is the wisdom of the Great Commandment, one that involves our whole person, 'heart, soul, mind and strength'. (Lk 10:25-29)

The wisdom Jesus reveals to us in the gospels is rooted in his Incarnation, for by becoming a human being he opens up for us an intimate knowledge of the love of God his Father. He immerses himself in our world and so we can come to know him within our own experience in exactly the same way we come to know the people who make love real or 'visible' for us.

> For I am certain of this ... no one will be able to come between us and the love of God made visible in Christ Jesus our Lord. (Rom 8:39)

When Jesus makes the love of God visible, he reveals it at the four levels at which all our experience comes. In other words, we can come to know God's love through our *senses* and *feelings*, through our capacity for *intuition* and for converting these intuitions into *convictions*. Because Jesus becomes a human being we can meet him in these four ways and thus accept the life-giving invitation of the Great Commandment to be loved and to love 'with our whole heart, soul, mind and strength'.

> Just then a lawyer stood up to test Jesus. 'Teacher,' he said, 'what must I do to inherit eternal life?' He said to him, 'What is written in the law? What do you read there?' He answered, 'You shall love the Lord your God with all your heart, and with all your soul, and with all your strength, and with all

your mind; and your neighbour as yourself.' And he said to him, 'You have given the right answer; do this, and you will live.' (Lk 10:25-28)

When we get our whole person involved in the way that the Great Commandment directs us to, we get an interior knowledge of 'the breadth and length and height and depth' of the love of Christ and thus of his wisdom.

> I pray that you may have the power to comprehend, with all the saints, what is the breadth and length and height and depth, and to know the love of Christ that surpasses knowledge, so that you may be filled with all the fullness of God. (Eph 3:18-19)

Because Jesus gives us an intimate knowledge of his love by mediating it through our senses and souls, through our hearts and minds, his wisdom becomes very real and relevant to our daily experience. His wisdom becomes *real* because when it comes to us through our senses and feelings it becomes concrete and visible, tangible and felt. (1 Jn 1:1-2) Since the wisdom of Jesus is expressed in human terms it also becomes *relevant* in the sense that it can speak to our daily experience rather than remaining in a spiritual realm remote from it. Because Jesus becomes incarnate all our experience of human love prolongs or is an extension of his incarnate love. The intimate knowledge Paul was given on the road to Damascus of how inseparable is the love of Christ from that of the Christian became the wisdom that inspired the rest of Paul's life. (Acts 9:3-6)

The growth of this wisdom we get through coming to know Jesus is so gradual that we are often unaware of its presence. It is a wisdom he would have us listen to and savour so that we might abide in it.

> As the Father has loved me, so I have loved you; abide in my love. If you keep my commandments, you will abide in my love, just as I have kept my Father's commandments and abide in his love. (Jn 15:9-10)

FEATURE 4

The role of traditional wisdom

We learn life's wisdom within a context provided by the family, the culture, the country and the church of which we are part. This context provides us with a broad field of experience, an accumulation of wisdom gathered over the centuries. Against the background of this universal experience, or traditional wisdom, we can interpret our much more limited personal experience. There is a vital interdependence between these two kinds of wisdom because traditional wisdom divorced from our personal wisdom can become irrelevant, while personal wisdom without that of the community can be foolish.

> The one who did not listen to the elders built a house without a door. (*Zambian proverb*)

In this feature we look at the role which the word and the Mass play in revealing how profound Jesus' love is. These two sources of Christian wisdom provide a context within which our own personal experience is given new meaning in the sense that we see our own experience in their light. If our experience is not seen in the light of Jesus' revelation in the word and in the Mass, the meaning and importance of everything is diminished. But the word and the Mass need our personal experience because if they do not address this they become less real and relevant.

We may think of the word of God as the main source of the revelation of God's love or wisdom. In the Bible, however, the works of God, such as the feeding of his people with manna in the desert, are an equally important source of God's revelation or wisdom. In the gospels, Jesus reveals his wisdom to us in the *words* he speaks as well as in the *deeds* he does. For example, in feeding the multitude (Jn 6:1-14) Jesus gives us a sign of his concern while in his death and resurrection he gives us the greatest revelation of this concern.

> When the people saw the sign that he had done, they began to say, 'This is indeed the prophet who is to come into the world.' (Jn 6:14) No one has greater love than this, to lay down one's life for one's friends. (Jn 15:13)

One of the most striking examples of the role of the word and the Mass in Jesus' self-revelation is given to us by Luke when he describes what took place when Jesus met his two dejected disciples on the road to Emmaus. He first of all invites them to tell him about their experience and only after listening to their story does he help them to discern it's true meaning in the light of the word of God and of 'the breaking of the bread'. Interpreting what has happened to them in this way has a powerful effect on them, for before Jesus met them they were sad and depressed but under the influence of the word and the 'breaking of the bread' they regained their former joy and enthusiasm.

> Then beginning with Moses and all the prophets, he interpreted to them the things about himself in all the scriptures ... They said to each other, 'Were not our hearts burning within us while he was talking to us on the road, while he was opening the scriptures to us?' ... Then they told what had happened on the road, and how he had been made known to them in the breaking of the bread. (Lk 24:17-35)

Though the word and the Mass satisfy our basic hunger in different ways they are mutually dependent sources of revelation. Where the word tells the story of the revelation of God's love, the Mass, as re-presenting the death and resurrection of Jesus, is the climax of that story. They both provide a wisdom that nourishes us as they both seek to keep alive the story of God's love. It is within this story that we find the wisdom that gives meaning and perspective to our own story.

> I am the living bread that came down from heaven. Whoever eats of this bread will live forever; and the bread that I will give for the life of the world is my flesh ... Those who eat my flesh and drink my blood abide in me, and I in them. (Jn 6:51, 56)

FEATURE 5

'Of his fullness we have received'

Generosity can take many forms as we can share to different degrees what we have but also who we are. Giving others a gift of ourselves in self-disclosure is an act of great generosity because of the effort involved in becoming aware of who we are, of putting words on this and then of sharing it. Making space to do this demands a disciplined effort to detach ourselves from the excessive demands of our outer world. To make this disciplined effort to give others this gift of ourselves in self-disclosure is a very loving thing to do for it involves an act of great trust if in this way we are to commit ourselves into the hands of others.

A striking feature of this portrait of Jesus is the generosity with which he shares his wisdom with us. He shares not only *all he has* but *all he is* with anyone who is willing to accept this gift of himself. He even wishes to share 'everything' he has heard from his Father, the full extent and depth of the intimacy they enjoy.

> I do not call you servants any longer, because the servant does not know what the master is doing; but I have called you friends, because I have made known to you everything that I have heard from my Father. (Jn 15:15)

Jesus sends us the Spirit to help us to explore what is involved in his sharing 'everything' about his relationship with his Father, their love and the union and joy that the beauty of this love draws them into.

> When the Spirit of truth comes, he will guide you into all the truth; for he will not speak on his own, but will speak whatever he hears, and he will declare to you the things that are to come. He will glorify me, because he will take what is mine and declare it to you. All that the Father has is mine. For this reason I said that he will take what is mine and declare it to you. (Jn 16:13-15)

In his parables Jesus uses the image of the banquet or the wedding feast to express the abundance of this life he wants to share with us. (Jn 10:10) The fact that it is a 'wedding feast' emphasises the intense love, intimacy and joy we are urged to enter. (Mt 22:1-10)

Another image of Jesus' generosity in sharing his wisdom with us is expressed in the book of Revelation where we are told that Jesus seeks to enter our inner room and to share our meal; this by his rich and gracious presence becomes a banquet.

> Listen! I am standing at the door, knocking; if you hear my voice and open the door, I will come in to you and eat with you, and you with me. (Rev 3:20)

The story of the feeding of the multitude is another expression of the generosity of Jesus. This is expressed in the number of people fed by Jesus and in the fact that they all had more than they could eat. (Mk 6:41-44) In all the gospel accounts of this event the Eucharistic symbolism is emphasised. This is particularly so of John who, after giving us an account of the feeding of the multitude, draws out at length the profound significance of this event. He describes how Jesus invites us to a banquet where he shares all he has and is with us: 'I am the bread of life. Whoever comes to me will never be hungry, and whoever believes in me will never be thirsty.' (Jn 6:35) Through the word of God (6:31-48) and through the bread of life Jesus satisfies our basic hunger in such a lavish way. (Jn 6:49-57) In speaking about eating his body and drinking his blood, John calls to mind the supreme moment of Jesus' generosity where he loves us to the extent of laying down his life for us: 'We know love by this, that he laid down his life for us.' (1 Jn 3:16)

The generosity of the way Jesus shares his wisdom with us is also highlighted by the word *peace*, as this word means a condition in which nothing is lacking. Jesus wants to share with us everything he shares with his Father. (Jn 15:15, Jn 1:16)

> I pray that you may ... know the love of Christ that surpasses knowledge, so that you may be filled with all the fullness of God. (Eph 3:18-19)

FEATURE 6

Engaging us in conversation

The wisdom we are contemplating in this portrait springs from an experience of being loved and from our efforts to respond to this love. The wisdom we get from this exchange is learned mainly in our relationships and more specifically through our ability to communicate within them. Those involved in a relationship initiate this communication by revealing something significant about themselves. They thus invite each other to listen and respond to this self-revelation. The depth of their relationship depends on how much of themselves they are willing to share and on their ability to listen and to respond to this.

In this feature we will look at how Jesus sees his life in terms of making his Father known to us and in terms of fostering our faith in this revelation. (Jn 17:26) This fostering of faith is seen by Jesus as 'the work of God' (Jn 6:29), as the food that sustains him. 'My food is to do the will of him who sent me and to complete his work.' (Jn 4:34)

Jesus fosters our faith mainly through conversation. To emphasise the importance of this, Jesus uses a dramatic event described in chapter 28 of the book of Genesis. There we are told of a dream Jacob had in which he saw a ladder stretching between heaven and earth and on it angels ascending and descending. Jesus sees himself as that ladder, as the focal point of communication between God and ourselves.

> And he said to him, 'Very truly, I tell you, you will see heaven opened and the angels of God ascending and descending upon the Son of Man.' (Jn 1:51)

The main way Jesus communicates his wisdom is through the dialogue he initiates with each person. We have an example of how he initiates this dialogue in the way he calls his disciples. Rather than giving them instructions on what is involved in following him, Jesus invites them to get to know him with his words, 'Come and see'. (Jn 1:35-39)

In order to communicate his wisdom to people, Jesus first listens to them, tuning in to where they are and to what they want. He is sensitive to what they seem ready to realise in their lives and helps them to do so. We have an example of how Jesus adjusts to where each person is in the way he calls Peter. (Lk 5:4-11) Jesus opens up a dialogue with each of us in which he tunes in to where we are and to what we are ripe for. What he wishes to reveal to us is discovered in coming to know him and the love of God for us that he makes visible.

We see how Jesus communicates his wisdom in the conversation he opens up with the Samaritan woman. He talks to her about her life, encouraging her to tell him about what she wants out of life and how she sees herself in the circumstances in which she lives. What impresses her in what he reveals to her about herself is the way that he accepts her and acknowledges her as worthy of his time and attention. He opens up a prospect of what she may become which is so exciting that she decides she must tell others about it.

> Then the woman left her water jar and went back to the city. She said to the people, 'Come and see a man who told me everything I have ever done! He cannot be the Messiah, can he?' They left the city and were on their way to him. (Jn 4:29-30)

It is in such a dialogue as he has with the Samaritan woman that Jesus communicates in a very gentle way who he is for us and who we are for him. He does this not just in words but mainly in the way he relates in a respectful, accepting and appreciative way that is full of concern for our welfare. In this very human way he is the 'wisdom of God'.

> We proclaim Christ crucified, a stumbling block to Jews and foolishness to Gentiles, but to those who are the called, both Jews and Greeks, Christ the power of God and the wisdom of God. (1 Cor 1:22-31)

Jesus proclaims this wisdom by giving us an interior knowledge of who we are for him. (Col 2:2-3)

FEATURE 7

Communicating assertively

We have been looking at a concept of wisdom which is born of an experience of being loved and of returning that love. This wisdom is had through relationships and through the way we communicate within these. If we are to carry on this communication effectively we are challenged to fulfil certain conditions. These centre around the willingness of people to listen and respond honestly to what they hear each other say. To do this, however, they need to make space to reflect on what they wish to share of themselves. To make the space necessary to communicate we need to free ourselves from being so dominated by the interests of our outer world that we have little time, energy and resources left for the relationships that are central to our inner world.

In this feature we look at a practical aspect of the wisdom of Jesus as he puts before us the concrete conditions of his being able to communicate with us. He challenges us to become aware of the wisdom he reveals to us and to take responsibility for developing the relationship with him which he seeks to initiate by this revelation.

> Why do you call me 'Lord, Lord,' and do not do what I tell you? I will show you what someone is like who comes to me, hears my words, and acts on them. That one is like a man building a house, who dug deeply and laid the foundation on rock; when a flood arose, the river burst against that house but could not shake it, because it had been well built. But the one who hears and does not act is like a man who built a house on the ground without a foundation. When the river burst against it, immediately it fell, and great was the ruin of that house.' (Lk 6:46-49)

Instead of accepting this challenge to take responsibility for developing and maintaining the relationship he seeks to initiate with us, we may drift down what Jesus calls 'the road to destruction'. (Mt 7:13-14) Jesus challenges us to choose the way to life by making a priority of developing the relationships which constitute our inner world. These are the relationships with him, with our inmost self, with others and with the whole of creation. If we are to develop these relationships we need to fulfil four basic conditions:

The first of these conditions is *freedom*. Jesus seeks this freedom for the rich young man when he invites him to free himself from the hold that his riches have on him. In this context riches is a general term covering all those attachments that enslave us. So the rich young man is invited to seek the freedom he needs to be with Jesus. (Mk 10:20-27)

When we attain freedom from whatever form riches take for us, we can then make *space* in our lives. Space is a generic term that covers such elements as the time, energy, and resources we need to make a priority of our main relationships. In the gospels a striking example of the way people find space in their lives when they become free is the man called Legion who has the time to listen to Jesus. (Mk 5:18-20)

The reason why Jesus wants to set us free from our demons is that we might make space in our lives to communicate with him. Our relationships will be as good as this communication, as good as the listening and the responding basic to this communication. Jesus takes the opportunity to make this point when he is told that his mother, who is on the fringe of the crowd he is addressing, wants to see him. He says that the closeness of our relationship with him is dependent on our willingness to communicate with him. (Lk 8:19-21)

A final condition of Jesus being able to communicate with us is that we learn to discern the signs of this communication all around us. We need to be aware of, to understand and respond to these signs through *reflection*.

> And becoming aware of it, Jesus said to them, 'Why are you talking about having no bread? Do you still not perceive or understand? Are your hearts hardened? Do you have eyes, and fail to see? Do you have ears, and fail to hear?' (Mk 8:17-18)

FEATURE 8

A capacity to delegate

We all know how hard it is to delegate work, the success of which is very important for us. Therefore, it is a very attractive quality in people when they give us something important to do and then leave us free to do it in our own way. This is especially true when they are aware that in delegating the work to us we may not have the competence to do it properly or in the way they would want it done. It requires magnanimity to make others plenipotentiaries and then to stand by our decision when we feel that those we have thus empowered to act on our behalf have not used this power in the way we wanted them to. It is, therefore, an enlivening experience when those who delegate work to us continue to trust us and to give us their full support in spite of the fact that we do not always honour their trust.

Jesus' capacity to take the risk of delegating his life's work to others shows itself right from the time he chooses his first disciples. For example, when he calls Peter he prepares him to be the one to whom he will entrust the work that he was sent to do by his Father. (Lk 5:8-11)

Jesus' capacity to delegate manifest itself in a number of striking ways. For example, when he sends Peter to do his Father's work, he is willing to leave him free to make mistakes. In delegating this work, the success of which meant everything to him, Jesus is magnanimous and continues to trust and support Peter even when Peter betrays that trust.

> When they had finished breakfast, Jesus said to Simon Peter, 'Simon son of John, do you love me more than these?' He said to him, 'Yes, Lord; you know that I love you.' Jesus said to him, 'Feed my lambs.' (Jn 21:15)

It is a very enlivening experience when those sending us to do some important work allow and even encourage us to do it in our own way. When I was young, it was very annoying when my father gave me a job to do and then kept checking out how I was doing it. Basic to the way Jesus delegates his own work to us is the freedom he leaves us to do it as we think best. After his resurrection, as he prepares his disciples for his departure from them, he purposely stands back to encourage them to take responsibility for continuing his work under the guidance of the Spirit. (Jn 16:7)

Closely associated with the freedom Jesus gives us is the trust he puts in us in giving us that freedom. He leaves us free to do things for ourselves and he trusts us to do them even though we may make mistakes. When Jesus sent out the twelve disciples he trusted them with his own work, with something that he felt passionately about.

> Then he went about among the villages teaching. He called the twelve and began to send them out two by two, and gave them authority over the unclean spirits ... So they went out and proclaimed that all should repent. They cast out many demons, and anointed with oil many who were sick and cured them. (Mk 6:7-13)

In spite of the fact that Jesus knows of the mistakes that his twelve disciples will make, he trusts them to act with his own authority, sending them out in the way he himself was sent out by his Father. 'As you have sent me into the world, so I have sent them into the world.' Jn 17:18) Jesus entrusts his disciples with the work of revealing the good news of God's love and providence and of fostering faith in it. This is a magnanimous thing to do when we consider how amateurish they were, as well as their lack of understanding of and loyalty to Jesus. (Mt 28:16-20) It is a real mystery of magnanimity when Jesus delegates his disciples to do even greater works than he himself has done. (Jn 14:12) When Jesus delegates his work to us and leaves us free to do it as we think best, he remains with us in a profoundly supportive way.

> They who have my commandments and keep them are those who love me; those who love me will be loved by my Father, and I will love them and reveal myself to them. (Jn 14:18-21)

THE SIXTH PORTRAIT

The faithful love of Jesus

We experience the love that characterises this portrait in people who are *faithful*, constant and steadfast in their relationships with us. Their fidelity emerges especially when we are disloyal or neglect our relationships with them. Our infidelity and neglect only seem to highlight the extent and depth of their *devotion* to developing and maintaining their relationships with us. The intensity of this devotion leads them to *sacrifice themselves* to preserve this relationship. The extent, depth and intensity of their devotion to others calls for *courage* if they are to maintain these relationships and make available the time, energy and resources required to do so.

What inspires the very obvious courage we notice in these people is their *deep conviction* that the world is in the hands of a loving providence. They are convinced that this providence has a plan for them, a dream which is implanted in their hearts. They have an inner *clarity* about how important this dream is and a decisiveness about the practical steps they need to take to realise it. A large part of the realisation of their dream has to do with the cultivation of relationships and there is a *warmth* about the way they conduct these. Once they have established these relationships with the people who are central to their lives, they have a deep desire to *include all*, especially those who live on the margins of society, in the warmth of their way of relating.

The features of the sixth portrait of Jesus

1. Jesus' love is *faithful*, constant and permanent in spite of the inconstancy of our relationship with him. His response to our infidelity is one of forgiveness and acceptance.

2. We see the extent and depth of this *devotion* of Jesus to each of us in the way, as the good shepherd, he continues to lead us into his love, in spite of the fact that we stray from the way he urges us to take.

3. In his devotion to us Jesus identifies with the *self-sacrificing* attitude of the Suffering Servant. From the time of his baptism, his life is dominated by his desire to sacrifice his life out of love for us.

4. Jesus' *courage* emerges as he faces those who oppose him and even want to kill him. On his journey to Jerusalem he faces his death with supreme courage, seeing it as part of his Father's loving plan for us.

5. All through his life Jesus *fosters our faith* in everything being part of the Father's provident plan. By his miracles he sets us free from our illusion that we live in a hostile world and from the fear this can cause.

6. His Father's provident plan gives Jesus *clarity and decisiveness*. We see this in the way he handles problems posed to him and in the discerning way he interprets the law.

7. There is a striking *warmth* about the way Jesus relates, even with those who have been disloyal or unfaithful to him. He seeks to draw these into an even more intimate relationship than before.

8. Jesus extends the intimacy he enjoys with his close friends to every person he meets. He is *at home with the outcast and sinner* in each of us.

FEATURE 1

One whose love is faithful

There is something to be treasured in friends who remain so over the years in spite of knowing our limitations. They do not let our infidelity obscure the goodness they would have us recognise and appreciate. Besides faithful we also use the words permanent, constant and enduring for this kind of love. Perhaps the most striking symbol of this love is the deep desire of two young people getting married as they solemnly pledge to each other a love that will outlast every hardship or difficulty and that will endure until their death.

A striking aspect of Jesus' love is how faithful, permanent, constant and enduring it is; it 'alters not with time's brief hours and weeks'. Jesus promises this even though he is conscious of our regular failure to work at and to maintain the relationship he initiates with us. In his parable about the sower Jesus describes how difficult it is for us to let his word strike deep and permanent roots in us. The parable is given a prominent place in the gospels as it faces one of the main themes of Jesus' life: the mystery of his fidelity in spite of the poor reception we give his efforts to make himself known to us.

> Listen! A sower went out to sow. And as he sowed, some seeds fell on the path, and the birds came and ate them up. Other seeds fell on rocky ground, where they did not have much soil, and they sprang up quickly, since they had no depth of soil. But when the sun rose, they were scorched; and since they had no root, they withered away. Other seeds fell among thorns, and the thorns grew up and choked them. Other seeds fell on good soil and brought forth grain, some a hundredfold, some sixty, some thirty. Let anyone with ears listen! (Mt 13:1-9)

Jesus *forgives* and accepts us and wants us to forgive and accept ourselves. He can be compared to a good friend whom we have offended and who does not want us to hold on to our guilt. As such he wants us to take the gift of his sacrament of reconciliation seriously. 'Receive the Holy Spirit. If you forgive the sins of any, they are forgiven them; if you retain the sins of any, they are retained.' (Jn 20:23)

Jesus 'is familiar with all our weakness' and he 'was tempted in every way that we are'. (Heb 4:15) This means that *he identifies with us in our weakness* and can empathise with us in our experience of it.

We have a concrete demonstration of Jesus' response to our infidelity in the way he deals with the sinful woman in Simon's house. Her presence is deeply offensive to Simon and his guests but Jesus, far from being embarrassed by her presence, is full of admiration for her courtesy towards him.

> Therefore, I tell you, her sins, which were many, have been forgiven; hence she has shown great love. But the one to whom little is forgiven, loves little. (Lk 7:44-50)

The response of Jesus, which may be the most difficult one for us to understand, is that he delights in and celebrates our return to him. What he celebrates is the predominantly good person he finds in us and this rather than our weakness is what he focuses on. He portrays his reaction to our infidelity in his parable of the lost sheep. It is a striking feature of this parable that each of the shepherd's sheep mean so much to him that he is prepared to leave the ninety-nine in order to search for the one which has strayed. Striking too is the delight he expresses when he finds his wayward sheep.

> So he told them this parable: 'Which one of you, having a hundred sheep and losing one of them, does not leave the ninety-nine in the wilderness and go after the one that is lost until he finds it? When he has found it, he lays it on his shoulders and rejoices. And when he comes home, he calls together his friends and neighbours, saying to them, 'Rejoice with me, for I have found my sheep that was lost.' Just so, I tell you, there will be more joy in heaven over one sinner who repents than over ninety-nine righteous persons who need no repentance. (Lk 15:3-7)

FEATURE 2

Jesus' devotion to his own

One of the ways that people's fidelity becomes apparent is in the extent and in the depth of their devotion to us. The extent of their devotion is seen in the constancy that characterises faithful love and this constancy is experienced in someone's tireless effort on our behalf over the years. The depth of their devotion is experienced when they continue in the relationships they have established with us even when we take their devotion for granted or are disloyal to them.

In describing the extent of his devotion to each person, Jesus returns to the image of the good shepherd that we find in Ezek 34:11-16. He uses this image to highlight how extensive is the good shepherd's care for his sheep.

> He calls his own sheep by name and leads them out. When he has brought out all his own, he goes ahead of them, and the sheep follow him because they know his voice. ... I am the gate. Whoever enters by me will be saved, and will come in and go out and find pasture. (Jn 10:4-18)

The depth of Jesus' devotion to us is shown by the way that he, as the good shepherd, leads us into life or to know himself and thus his Father just as they know each other. This is what Jesus spends his life doing as he leads us into his own relationship with his Father.

> I came that they may have life, and have it abundantly. I am the good shepherd. I know my own and my own know me, just as the Father knows me and I know the Father. And I lay down my life for the sheep. I have other sheep that do not belong to this fold. I must bring them also, and they will listen to my voice. So there will be one flock, one shepherd. (Jn 10:10-14)

Leading us into this profound relationship is for Jesus his Father's will, the centre of his concern, the food that sustains him. 'My food is to do the will of him who sent me and to complete his work.' (Jn 4:34) 'I have come down from heaven, not to do my own will, but the will of him who sent me.' (Jn 6:38) Since in the past we may have been inclined to think of the will of God as distinct from our deepest dream, it is important that we see his will as identical with what Paul calls 'our sanctification' or with our deepest needs and desires. 'For this is the will of God, your sanctification.' (1 Thes 4:3) Jesus devotes himself to fostering our faith as it is this that realises our deepest dream or satisfies our essential hunger. 'I am the bread of life. Whoever comes to me will never be hungry, and whoever believes in me will never be thirsty.' (Jn 6:35)

We are given a very clear example of the depth of Jesus' devotion in the way his relationship with Peter evolves. He calls Peter by name (Lk 5:1-11) and gives him a role of immense responsibility. (Lk 9:18-21) Jesus is willing to sustain his intimacy with him in spite of the fact that he foresees Peter's denial of him.

> Simon, Simon, listen! Satan has demanded to sift all of you like wheat, but I have prayed for you that your own faith may not fail; and you, when once you have turned back, strengthen your brothers. (Lk 22:31-34)

It is when Jesus meets Peter by the lakeside after the resurrection that his devotion to him is most touchingly portrayed. In spite of Peter's gross disloyalty, Jesus does not withdraw from him but reinstates him in his former position of leadership in a way that gives Peter a chance to match his threefold denial with a threefold act of acceptance of Jesus' forgiveness. 'He said to him the third time, 'Simon son of John, do you love me?' … And he said to him, 'Lord, you know everything; you know that I love you.' Jesus said to him, 'Feed my sheep.' (Jn 21:15-18) This portrayal of Jesus' fidelity is strikingly similar to God's fidelity to us as it is portrayed in the parable of the prodigal son.

> The father said to his slaves, 'Quickly, bring out a robe – the best one – and put it on him; put a ring on his finger and sandals on his feet. And get the fatted calf and kill it, and let us eat and celebrate.' (Lk 15:21-24)

FEATURE 3

'He loved me and sacrificed himself for me'

In this feature we look at how the intensity of our devotion to others is expressed when we sacrifice ourselves for them. The intensity of the sacrifice may not always be obvious as it can involve a lifetime of inconspicuous service of others in which we make our time and our resourcefulness available to them. We notice this capacity of people to give their time, energy and resourcefulness for the good of others in the daily sacrifices parents make to give their children a good start in life. We also notice this capacity for self-sacrifice in our experiences of how unselfish people can be when they put their lives at risk for those for whom they have a deep affection. This self-sacrificing devotion is particularly striking when it is expressed in an unconditional, inconspicuous and even joyful way.

This capacity for self-sacrificing devotion is exemplified in the Old Covenant by the Suffering Servant. In the prophet Isaiah this person is described as one who takes on the sufferings of others and thereby heals and saves them. (Is 53:5-7) At his baptism Jesus identifies with the Suffering Servant – the name 'Son' addressed to him there also means 'Servant'. Throughout his public life Jesus sees himself fulfilling this role. 'This is my Son, the Beloved, with whom I am well pleased.' (Mt 3:16-17)

This image of Jesus as the Suffering Servant is one that pervades the gospels.

> For who is greater, the one who is at the table or the one who serves? Is it not the one at the table? But I am among you as one who serves. (Lk 22:27)

Jesus sees himself as one who serves us to the point of sacrificing himself for us. What he says and does throughout the second half of his public life is dominated by his journey to Jerusalem.

> Jesus went through one town and village after another, teaching as he made his way to Jerusalem. (Lk 13:22)

What will happen to Jesus in Jerusalem is repeatedly predicted in the gospels; he will suffer, be put to death and rise again.

Jesus foresees his fate not only as his own fate but also as that of anyone who wishes to follow him.

> The Son of Man must undergo great suffering, and be rejected by the elders, chief priests, and scribes, and be killed, and on the third day be raised. Then he said to them all, 'If any want to become my followers, let them deny themselves and take up their cross daily and follow me. For those who want to save their life will lose it, and those who lose their life for my sake will save it.' (Lk 9:21-25)

In the parable of the good shepherd Jesus draws out the reasons why he sacrifices himself for those he loves.

> I am the good shepherd. The good shepherd lays down his life for the sheep. ... For this reason the Father loves me, because I lay down my life in order to take it up again. No one takes it from me, but I lay it down of my own accord. I have power to lay it down, and I have power to take it up again. (Jn 10:11-13, 17-18)

In his gospel John identifies Jesus' ultimate motive for undertaking his passion and death as a love that knows no limits. The words John uses to describe this love can mean that Jesus loved us 'to the utmost extent', 'to death' or 'to the end'. (Jn 13:1) Paul also sees Jesus as one who sacrifices himself, not just for people in general, but for each individual person. 'And the life I now live in the flesh I live by faith in the Son of God, who loved me and gave himself for me.' (Gal 2:20) Jesus gives us the Mass to keep alive the memory of himself as one who sacrifices all in his supreme act of love for us.

> Then he took a loaf of bread, and when he had given thanks, he broke it and gave it to them, saying, 'This is my body, which is given for you. Do this in remembrance of me.' And he did the same with the cup after supper, saying, 'This cup that is poured out for you is the new covenant in my blood.' (Lk 22:19-20)

FEATURE 4

The courage of Jesus

Devotion to others calls for courage at a number of levels. For example, courage is needed to initiate, establish and maintain the basic relationships of our lives, with God, with our inner selves and with others. Courage is also required when our devotion to others lasts over a long period in which constant demands are made on our time and energy. Again courage is called for when we take risks in dangerous situations on behalf of others. Finally, there is a further level of courage needed when our lives are endangered because we take a stand in defence of others.

Courage characterises the life of Jesus. It is a courage that is called for during his public life as the opposition to him grows and the Pharisees plan to kill him.

> Again he entered the synagogue, and a man was there who had a withered hand. They watched him to see whether he would cure him on the Sabbath, so that they might accuse him. And he said to the man who had the withered hand, 'Come forward.' Then he said to them, 'Is it lawful to do good or to do harm on the Sabbath, to save life or to kill?' But they were silent. He looked around at them with anger; he was grieved at their hardness of heart and said to the man, 'Stretch out your hand.' He stretched it out, and his hand was restored. The Pharisees went out and immediately conspired with the Harridans against him, how to destroy him. (Mk 3:1-6)

Jesus is aware of all the shades of unbelief he faces and even of the desire of some people to kill him. However, he never allows himself to be intimidated by those who oppose him. People are amazed at the fact that in spite of the plans of the Jews to kill him, Jesus continues to speak out openly.

> The world cannot hate you, but it hates me because I testify against it that its works are evil ... Now some of the people of Jerusalem were saying, 'Is not this the man whom they are trying to kill? And here he is, speaking openly, but they say

nothing to him!' (Jn 7:7, 25-26)

Throughout the second half of the gospel story, Jesus resolutely journeys towards Jerusalem even though he knows the sufferings and death that await him there. He undertakes this journey largely on his own for even his disciples, doubting the wisdom of what he is doing, fail to support him and even try to get him to change course.

> Then he began to teach them that the Son of Man must undergo great suffering, and be rejected by the elders, the chief priests, and the scribes, and be killed, and after three days rise again. He said all this quite openly. And Peter took him aside and began to rebuke him. But turning and looking at his disciples, he rebuked Peter and said, 'Get behind me, Satan! For you are setting your mind not on divine things but on human things.' (Mk 8:31-33)

It is in facing his passion and death that the courage of Jesus emerges most clearly. During his agony in the garden Jesus does not hide his fear and yet in spite of being immersed in the sufferings he is about to undergo he faces them in a calm and courageous way. (Mk 14:32-37) John's records the dignified courage of Jesus as he faces his arrest with majestic calm. (Jn 18:1-9)

The source of Jesus' courage is his abiding consciousness of how his suffering and death are part of his Father's loving plan of salvation. (Jn 19:30) The mainspring of Jesus' courage is his certainty of the all-encompassing care of his Father.

> And when Jesus had cried with a loud voice, he said, 'Father, into thy hands I commend my spirit': and having said this, he breathed his last. (Lk 23:46) When Jesus had received the wine, he said, 'It is finished.' Then he bowed his head and gave up his spirit. (Jn 19:30)

FEATURE 5

Jesus fosters faith

In this and the next feature we will reflect on our experience of people who are devoted to our basic interests. The first of these interests is that we develop a healthy view of our world and the second is that we become clear and decisive about how we evaluate all in the light of this worldview and live consistently with it. We get a glimpse of the first of these from people who inspire and foster our faith in a world that is a secure and friendly place to live because it is governed by a loving providence. Even though we are 'mote-like' within this all-encompassing, profound and abiding providence, we each have our unique place in it.

> Thee, God, I come from, to thee go,
> All day long I like fountain flow
> From thy hand out, swayed about
> Mote-like in thy mighty glow.
> *(G. M. Hopkins)*

Jesus spends his life inspiring and fostering faith. He goes around proclaiming the 'good news' and opening up a vision of the world that centres on God's providence and on the love that inspires it. 'The Spirit of the Lord is upon me, because he has anointed me to bring good news to the poor.' (Lk 4:18)

Jesus works miracles to inspire faith in God's providence. These miracles are signs of the compassion of Jesus for wounded humanity and it is faith in his compassion that heals people at the deepest level.

> He said to her, 'Daughter, your faith has made you well; go in peace.' While he was still speaking, someone came from the leader's house to say, 'Your daughter is dead; do not trouble the teacher any longer.' When Jesus heard this, he replied, 'Do not fear. Only believe, and she will be saved.' (Lk 8:48-50)

The illusion that we live in a hostile world is directly opposed to the belief that the world is pervaded by a loving providence. This illusion manifests itself in the fear that always accompanies it. When Jesus notices fear he counters it by an appeal to our faith in the fact that he is always with us. For example, during the storm on the lake when the disciples are in danger of succumbing to fear, Jesus appears and assures them of his presence, using those words so frequently repeated in the Old Testament, 'Do not be afraid for I am with you.'

> When evening came, his disciples went down to the sea, got into a boat, and started across the sea to Capernaum. It was now dark, and Jesus had not yet come to them. The sea became rough because a strong wind was blowing. When they had rowed about three or four miles, they saw Jesus walking on the sea and coming near the boat, and they were terrified. But he said to them, 'It is I; do not be afraid.' Then they wanted to take him into the boat, and immediately the boat reached the land toward which they were going. (Jn 6:16-21)

Jesus' work of inspiring faith is symbolised by his opening the eyes of those who are blind. He wants to open their eyes to what is for him the basic vision of reality, to what he calls the good news. It is in the light of this good news or of the reality of God's love and providence that he wants us to see the world around us.

> Jesus laid his hands on his eyes again; and he looked intently and his sight was restored, and he saw everything clearly. (Mk 8:22-26)

Jesus asks us to believe that all that surrounds us in the universe is there to nourish us. Everything that happens, therefore, even the most adverse things, 'work together onto good for those who love God'. (Rom 8:28) How pervasive this providence of God is for Jesus can be judged from the following passage.

> But if God so clothes the grass of the field, which is alive today and tomorrow is thrown into the oven, how much more will he clothe you, you of little faith! (Lk 12:22-32)

FEATURE 6

The clarity and decisiveness of Jesus

People like our parents not only inspire and foster in us a way of seeing the world around us but they also urge us to be true to this worldview by giving it practical expression in the way we live. With time we develop our own deep convictions and we feel called to live consistently with these. Our consciences tell us what are the implications of our beliefs and what it means to walk in the light of these beliefs. However, the vision faith inspires in us can grow dim or we may not take responsibility for walking in the light of it. When this happens we can become confused and indecisive. Sometimes a dark period in our life challenges us to discern what we believe in and what we should do to live consistently with what we believe. Our faith can thus challenge us to light a candle rather than to curse the darkness.

Since Jesus is a divine person we may take his clarity of thought and the decisiveness with which he acts for granted. This will be so, especially if we fail to take the Incarnation seriously and the fact that Jesus grew in 'wisdom and in years' in the way that any human being grows.

> Then he went down with them and came to Nazareth, and was obedient to them. His mother treasured all these things in her heart. And Jesus increased in wisdom and in years, and in divine and human favour. (Lk 2:51-52)

Even though Jesus is a comparatively young person at the beginning of his public life, we see his clarity and decisiveness in the way he challenges us in his parables to take responsibility for living consistently with what we believe. We see this clarity in his convictions about what is true and worthwhile and what it means to walk in the light of these convictions. We also see Jesus' clarity and sureness in the way he handles the objections of the Jews to his disciples plucking and eating grain on the Sabbath.

> Have you not read in the law that on the Sabbath the priests in the temple break the Sabbath and yet are guiltless? I tell you, something greater than the temple is here. But if you had known what this means, 'I desire mercy and not sacri-

fice,' you would not have condemned the guiltless. For the Son of Man is lord of the Sabbath. (Mt 12:1-8)

Jesus' sureness about what is consistent with his vision is seen when, on the Sabbath, he heals the man with the withered hand. We see this sureness also in the forceful way that Jesus exposes the inconsistency in the law which does not allow one to do for humans what one is allowed to do for animals.

> He left that place and entered their synagogue; a man was there with a withered hand, and they asked him, 'Is it lawful to cure on the Sabbath?' so that they might accuse him. He said to them, 'Suppose one of you has only one sheep and it falls into a pit on the Sabbath; will you not lay hold of it and lift it out? How much more valuable is a human being than a sheep! So it is lawful to do good on the Sabbath.' Then he said to the man, 'Stretch out your hand.' He stretched it out, and it was restored, as sound as the other. But the Pharisees went out and conspired against him, how to destroy him. (Mt 12:9-14)

Jesus shows an amazing clarity about his own relationship with his Father and with the Spirit, as well as about the precise nature of our relationship with each of them. In a brief statement in John's gospel he describes these relationships in a way that is clear and profound.

> I still have many things to say to you, but you cannot bear them now. When the Spirit of truth comes, he will guide you into all the truth; for he will not speak on his own, but will speak whatever he hears, and he will declare to you the things that are to come. He will glorify me, because he will take what is mine and declare it to you. All that the Father has is mine. For this reason I said that he will take what is mine and declare it to you. (Jn 16:12-15)

FEATURE 7

The warmth with which Jesus relates

In features 5 and 6 we looked at how people pass on to us a way of seeing the world around us and urge us to be clear and decisive in living out of this view of the world. While it is important that we take responsibility for our lives as individuals in this way it is equally important, as we will see in features 7 and 8, that we take responsibility for the way we relate with others, that we learn to love others as we love ourselves. In this present feature we will look at how we take responsibility for establishing and maintaining warm relationships with others. This is not easy, as we have a strong tendency to distance ourselves from people who are disloyal to us or who neglect our relationship with them. We may relate with them in a cool, detached and formal way and though we may be outwardly courteous towards them our heart is not in the courtesy. People who are able to overcome this distance and coldness and maintain a warm relationship with others who have let them down are to be admired and treasured.

There is a striking warmth about the way Jesus responds to our infidelity. He does not withdraw from us when we are disloyal to him but he seeks to restore the intimacy which has been lost. He takes the initiative in seeking to mend our relationships with him when these have been impaired by our failure to give the time, energy and resources needed to maintain them. This capacity of Jesus to maintain the warmth of his relationship with us, in spite of our infidelity, is symbolised in the parable he told about the lost sheep.

> Which one of you, having a hundred sheep and losing one of them, does not leave the ninety-nine in the wilderness and go after the one that is lost until he finds it? When he has found it, he lays it on his shoulders and rejoices. And when he comes home, he calls together his friends and neighbours, saying to them, 'Rejoice with me, for I have found my sheep that was lost.' Just so, I tell you, there will be more joy in heaven over one sinner who repents than over ninety-nine righteous persons who need no repentance. (Lk 15:4-7)

When Jesus gathers his disciples together to celebrate the Passover meal, there is a great warmth about what he does. It is moving that he draws them to him in spite of the fact that among them there is one who conspires to bring about his death, and others who will deny and desert him when he most needs their support. (Lk 22:7-13) We find a striking expression of the enduring quality of the warmth of Jesus' loyalty when he appears to his disciples at the lakeside after his resurrection. Even though they abandoned him in his hour of need when he had begged them to be with him, he seeks them out and treats them with deference and a gentleness that we can only wonder at.

> When they had gone ashore, they saw a charcoal fire there, with fish on it, and bread. Jesus said to them, 'Bring some of the fish that you have just caught.' So Simon Peter went aboard and hauled the net ashore, full of large fish, a hundred fifty-three of them; and though there were so many, the net was not torn. Jesus said to them, 'Come and have breakfast.' Now none of the disciples dared to ask him, 'Who are you?' because they knew it was the Lord. Jesus came and took the bread and gave it to them, and did the same with the fish. This was now the third time that Jesus appeared to the disciples after he was raised from the dead. (Jn 21:9-14)

Jesus does not pass us by on the road when he finds us deeply wounded by our sinfulness and in this way he is the original Good Samaritan. (Lk 10:33-34) We see how he is full of sensitive and warm compassion when he meets two of his disciples on the road to Emmaus. They are in great pain about the passion and death of Jesus and are sad and in despair. Jesus listens to the story of their suffering and then helps them see what has happened in the consoling light of his word and of all that is symbolised by 'the breaking of bread'. The warm compassion of the Good Samaritan turns their sadness to joy and their despair to enthusiasm. (Lk 24:15-32)

FEATURE 8

At home with the outcast and the sinner

It is one thing to establish and maintain warm relationships with those who form the immediate circle of our family and friends but it is much more demanding to welcome a wider range of people into the circle of our warm relationships. It is a fact, however, that when we learn to establish warm relationships with a small number of people, our capacity to take others into this warm environment is increased.

When Jesus speaks to his disciples at the last supper he knows they will betray, deny and abandon him. In spite of this he wants them to believe that their gross disloyalty will not cut them off from the intimacy he and the Father seek to share with them.

> Those who love me will keep my word, and my Father will love them, and we will come to them and make our home with them. (Jn 14:23)

Jesus' attitude to the weak and wayward is illustrated by his desire to eat with people who are considered to be sinners and outcasts. It is at a feast to celebrate his choice of one of these people as his disciple that Jesus defends his desire to befriend the sinners and outcasts of society.

> As Jesus was walking along, he saw a man called Matthew sitting at the tax booth; and he said to him, 'Follow me.' And he got up and followed him. And as he sat at dinner in the house, many tax collectors and sinners came and were sitting with him and his disciples. When the Pharisees saw this, they said to his disciples, 'Why does your teacher eat with tax collectors and sinners?' But when he heard this, he said, 'Those who are well have no need of a physician, but those who are sick. Go and learn what this means, "I desire mercy, not sacrifice." For I have come to call not the righteous but sinners.' (Mt 9:9-13)

Zacchaeus is also an outcast and highly unpopular with the crowd. Yet it is Zacchaeus above anyone else in the crowd that Jesus chooses to eat with and thus to befriend.

'Zacchaeus, hurry and come down; for I must stay at your house today.' So he hurried down and was happy to welcome him. All who saw it began to grumble and said, 'He has gone to be the guest of one who is a sinner.' Zacchaeus stood there and said to the Lord, 'Look, half of my possessions, Lord, I will give to the poor; and if I have defrauded anyone of anything, I will pay back four times as much.' Then Jesus said to him, 'Today salvation has come to this house, because he too is a son of Abraham. For the Son of Man came to seek out and to save the lost.' (Lk 19:5-10)

Even though Jesus wants to befriend the scribes and Pharisees in the way he befriends Matthew and Zacchaeus, he is not able to do this as they lack the openness required for such an intimate relationship. They lack the poverty of spirit or the spirit of the Beatitudes that forms the basis of such an intimate relationship with God. It is only to the poor of spirit that the kingdom of God belongs. 'Blessed are the poor in spirit, for theirs is the kingdom of heaven.' (Mt 5:1-12) In the book of Revelation this poverty of spirit is seen as a willingness to accept that we are 'wretched, pitiable, poor, blind, and naked' and this attitude is fundamental to intimacy with Jesus or for sharing table fellowship with him.

For you say, 'I am rich, I have prospered, and I need nothing.' You do not realize that you are wretched, pitiable, poor, blind, and naked. Therefore I counsel you to buy from me gold refined by fire so that you may be rich; and white robes to clothe you and to keep the shame of your nakedness from being seen; and salve to anoint your eyes so that you may see. I reprove and discipline those whom I love. Be earnest, therefore, and repent. Listen! I am standing at the door, knocking; if you hear my voice and open the door, I will come in to you and eat with you, and you with me. To the one who conquers I will give a place with me on my throne, just as I myself conquered and sat down with my Father on his throne. Let anyone who has an ear listen to what the Spirit is saying to the churches.' (Rev 3:17-22)

A joyful love

We catch a glimpse of this portrait in the love of those whose lives are characterised by *joy*. We find that these people often have a deep desire *to share their joy* as they realise that it is as important for others as it is for themselves. Since joy is so important for them, their deepest wish for others is that they would be *completely happy*.

We often find that the people whose joy pervades their lives base it on *a holistic or all inclusive vision*. This allows them to live happily with their limitations and weaknesses as well as with the gifted and graced person they find in themselves and in others. Adopting this holistic vision involves the *disciplined effort* to bring about the change of mind and heart required if they are to develop the conviction of being loved on which their happiness rests.

People whose lives are characterised by joy are usually good at *overcoming the threat to their happiness that weaknesses and failures pose*. They also have a facility in overcoming the depressing effects of life's hardships, being good at *regaining their joy* when they find themselves in poor spirits. Finally, the joy of those who give us a realistic picture of this kind of love is a *quiet or sober* one that has its source in a balanced mixture of joy that comes to us through the different levels at which we relate, through sense and soul, through heart and mind.

The features of the seventh portrait of Jesus

1. Jesus' intimate knowledge of his Father's love is the ultimate source of his *joy* and of that which he wants to share with us.

2. Jesus has an intense *desire to share his joy* with us. He compares this deep joy that comes from an interior knowledge of his Father's love to a banquet which he urges us to come to.

3. Jesus wants our happiness to be as *complete and constant* as is the love of God which is its source. He seeks to maintain the joy that comes from this revelation by the word of God and the Mass.

4. Jesus' joy depends on a *vision* more than on people and circumstances. It is a constructive and consoling vision that sees life's limitations and suffering in the context of God's gifts and grace.

5. Adopting this vision that faith gives us involves *a difficult change of mind and heart* that Jesus compares to dying. It takes time, energy and resourcefulness to let Jesus' love and its joy engage our whole person.

6. Joy for Jesus involves *being reconciled* with all the parts of ourselves we have become estranged from. He highlights all the good that is in and around us so that we might see all else from this perspective.

7. When we do lose this perspective and as a result our enthusiasm and our joy, Jesus seeks to restore these as he did for his two disciples on the road to Emmaus.

8. The joy Jesus invites us to share involves immersing our whole person, senses and soul, heart and mind, in his love. The joy that emerges from doing this is a *quiet, profound and pervasive* one.

FEATURE 1

The joy that characterises Jesus' life

There are very different attitudes to joy or happiness and it is important to become aware of what attitude we adopt, as this will determine how much joy or happiness we are open to. For example, we might see joy as central to life and thus be at home with the belief that we are made for joy, or we might think of joy as periperal and not to be sought or expected as an essential part of human life. Again we may *think* one way about joy but *feel* quite differently about it. Intellectually we may go along with the view that life is meant to be enjoyed and at the same time we may have reservations about making it so central in practice. In our mind we may go along with Aristotle's dictum that we are active to be leisurely but feel in our bones that we are leisurely to be active.

A deep joy pervades the life of Jesus. This joy is very obvious at the beginning of his life and in the resurrection scenes. In a less conspicuous way it pervades everything he says and does, as 'complete' joy is central to his revelation of his Father to us. 'I have said these things to you so that my joy may be in you, and that your joy may be complete.' (Jn 15:11)

In his *Theology of the Old Testament* Eichrodt holds that when we compare the Old Testament with other religious books of the time the prevalence of joy is one of its most distinct characteristics. This prevalence of joy is even more striking in the gospels. In the early chapters of St Luke's gospel, Jesus' coming is described as an event which is enveloped in intense joy.

> You will have joy and gladness, and many will rejoice at his birth (Lk 1:28) ... For as soon as I heard the sound of your greeting, the child in my womb leaped for joy. And Mary said (Lk 1:44) ... 'My soul magnifies the Lord, and my spirit rejoices in God my Saviour (Lk 1:47) ... Her neighbours and relatives heard that the Lord had shown his great mercy to her, and they rejoiced with her (Lk 1:58) ... But the angel said to them, 'Do not be afraid; for see, I am bringing you good

news of great joy for all the people. (Lk 2:10)

The joy that surrounds Jesus' coming among us is symbolised by Matthew's story of the Magi. They come from afar following this light or the star and they are 'overwhelmed with joy' when it leads them to Jesus. (Mt 2:10)

Jesus works his first miracle at a wedding feast where he changes water into wine. It is significant that he first manifests his glory in this simple act of kindness by which he provides a plentiful supply of what in a very sensate way gladdens our hearts. (Jn 2:1-11) The wedding feast at Cana picks up a theme of joy from the Old Testament where God's delight is compared to that of a bridegroom rejoicing in his bride. Jesus is fulfilling his role as the revelation in human terms of the capacity of God to celebrate, to be joyful and to delight in each of us. 'As the bridegroom rejoices over the bride, so shall your God rejoice over you.' (Is 62:4-5) Luke testifies that Jesus radiates this joy in 'all the wonderful things' he does.

> When he said this, all his opponents were put to shame; and the entire crowd was rejoicing at all the wonderful things that he was doing. (Lk 13:17)

It is by his passion, death and resurrection that Jesus gives us the fullest expression of what is the ultimate source of our joy. (Jn 15:11) It is this joy and peace that pervades the resurrection scenes. 'While in their joy they were disbelieving and still wondering, he said to them, "Have you anything here to eat?" ... And they worshipped him, and returned to Jerusalem with great joy.' (Lk 24:41, 52) Paul sees the peace and joy which Jesus brings to be so central to Christianity that he identifies it with the kingdom of God. (Rom 14:17) The deepest source of Jesus' joy, as well as of ours, is his willingness to 'abide in' the love the Father has for him.

> As the Father has loved me, so I have loved you; abide in my love. If you keep my commandments, you will abide in my love, just as I have kept my Father's commandments and abide in his love. I have said these things to you so that my joy may be in you, and that your joy may be complete. (Jn 15:9-11)

FEATURE 2

'That you might share my joy'

We might readily agree that sharing our happiness with others is a good thing but we may not see it as central to what life is all about. Our attitude to sharing our joy with others may be revealed in the way we react to people who bring a spirit of light heartedness to where we work. We may see people who make a priority of being joyful and of sharing it as running counter to the serious business of work. We might ask ourselves if our experience of those we work for is of people with an agenda of things to be done or of people who make our enjoyment of what we do a priority. It might be interesting to see how we would react to something like the following being said to us or whether we would consider it to be an important thing to say to those we love.

> Think of me kindly and rest assured that no one would more rejoice to hear of your happiness. *(Ludwig van Beethoven)*

Jesus has an intense desire to share his joy with us. This desire is essential to the main aim of Jesus' life which is to make the Father's love known to us. We could even say that the purpose of this revelation is to share his own joy with us. 'I have said these things to you so that my joy may be in you, and that your joy may be complete.' (Jn 15:11) '

> I speak these things in the world so that they may have my joy made complete in themselves. (Jn 17:13)

Jesus uses the symbol of a banquet (Lk 14:15-24) and of a wedding feast (Mt 22:1-10) to express the abundance of the joy he wants us to make our own of.

> Someone gave a great dinner and invited many. At the time for the dinner he sent his slave to say to those who had been invited, 'Come; for everything is ready now.' But they all alike began to make excuses. The first said to him, 'I have bought a piece of land, and I must go out and see it; please accept my regrets.' Another said, 'I have bought five yoke of oxen, and I am going to try them out; please accept my regrets.' Another said, 'I have just been married, and therefore I can-

not come.' So the slave returned and reported this to his master. Then the owner of the house became angry and said to his slave, 'Go out at once into the streets and lanes of the town and bring in the poor, the crippled, the blind, and the lame.' And the slave said, 'Sir, what you ordered has been done, and there is still room.' Then the master said to the slave, 'Go out into the roads and lanes, and compel people to come in, so that my house may be filled. For I tell you, none of those who were invited will taste my dinner.' (Lk 14:15-24)

The banquet symbolises the peace which Jesus aims to give us as his own special gift. 'Peace I leave with you; my peace I give to you. I do not give to you as the world gives.' (Jn 14:27) The word *peace* has a meaning that is distinctive to the Bible. In John McKenzie's *Dictionary of the Bible* it is defined as 'the fullness of all good things' and the *Jerusalem Bible* says that in the gospel it means the perfect happiness that Jesus as the Messiah brings. This peace, joy or happiness permeates the resurrection scenes and the Acts of the Apostles.

When it was evening on that day, the first day of the week, and the doors of the house where the disciples had met were locked for fear of the Jews, Jesus came and stood among them and said, 'Peace be with you.' After he said this, he showed them his hands and his side. Then the disciples rejoiced when they saw the Lord. (Jn 20:19-20)

When Jesus sends out the 72 disciples he tells them to share the gift of peace that he has given them. Their wish for those they meet on their journey is to be a peace they themselves will experience in their efforts to bring the good news to others.

Whatever house you enter, first say, 'Peace to this house!' ... The seventy two returned with joy ... At that same hour Jesus rejoiced in the Holy Spirit ... Blessed (happy) are the eyes that see what you see! For I tell you that many prophets and kings desired to see what you see, but did not see it, and to hear what you hear, but did not hear it. (Lk 10:1-20)

FEATURE 3

'That your happiness may be complete'

People who want to make our complete happiness a priority may seem unrealistic. This could be because we have much lower expectations of the happiness life should bring us than they have. Again we may expect life to be difficult and conclude that complete happiness in this life is an unrealistic expectation. The fact that, for a large percentage of the world's population, life is a struggle to survive may make any idea of our being made for happiness seem naïve. This will be particularly so if we associate happiness and material prosperity. Being conscious that so many people have not much of this world's goods may make us feel bad about the fact that we have so much. So rather than feel grateful for the good things we enjoy we may find them tinged with guilt. We may find it hard to harmonise our experience of the harshness of life for many people with the following:

> I will ponder with much affection how much God our Lord has done for me, and how much he has given me of what he has, and finally, how much, as far as he can, the same Lord desires to give Himself to me according to his divine plan. (*The Spiritual Exercises* No 234)

Jesus wants us to be 'completely' happy and he plans to bring this about by revealing himself to each person willing to accept this gift. He says to each of us what he said to his first disciples, 'Come and see.' (John 1:38-39) In coming to know Jesus we attain an intimate knowledge of his Father's love for us and this above all else is the source of the 'complete' happiness Jesus promises us. 'As the Father has loved me, so I have loved you; abide in my love … I have said these things to you so that my joy may be in you, and that your joy may be complete.' (Jn 15:11) 'The supreme happiness is the conviction of being loved.' (*Victor Hugo*)

We get used to the reality that in life we can only expect to get what we earn, what we achieve through our own effort. In the parable of the labourers in the vineyard, Jesus invites us to accept the reality that what God offers us is Grace, a gift given freely and in abundance. (Mt 20:1-16) The extent and depth of this generosity is expressed for us by Paul in his prayer that we would 'know the love of Christ ... and be filled with all the fullness of God'.

> I pray that you may have the power to comprehend, with all the saints, what is the breadth and length and height and depth, and to know the love of Christ that surpasses knowledge, so that you may be filled with all the fullness of God. (Eph 3:16-19)

The fullness of God's love that Jesus desires to share with us, and the joy that this opens up for us, is symbolised in the story of how Jesus fed the multitude. In the way these stories are told it is clear that they look back to the feeding of the people in the desert with manna and that they also look forward to the Mass. Therefore, in the context in which these stories are told, they are richly symbolic of the abundance of peace, joy and happiness which Jesus wishes to share with us.

> Taking the five loaves and the two fish, he looked up to heaven, and blessed and broke the loaves, and gave them to his disciples to set before the people; and he divided the two fish among them all. And all ate and were filled; and they took up twelve baskets full of broken pieces and of the fish. Those who had eaten the loaves numbered five thousand men. (Mk 6:39-44)

In John's account of the feeding of the multitude Jesus explains the significance of what he has done in terms of the word of God and of his body and blood. Both are described by Jesus as food which will satisfy our essential hunger for his love and for the peace, joy and happiness which belief in this love brings us.

> I am the bread of life. Whoever comes to me will never be hungry, and whoever believes in me will never be thirsty. (Jn 6:35)

> I speak these things in the world so that they may have my joy made complete in themselves. (Jn 17:13)

FEATURE 4

'Happy are you because you see'

There is a belief among psychologists that it is not people or circumstances that make us unhappy but the way we think about or see things. This belief is dramatically expressed by the poet John Milton.

> The mind is its own place and in itself
> Can make a heaven of hell, a hell of heaven.

The vision on which our happiness depends is a holistic one in the sense that it incorporates the two basic realities of our poverty and of our potential, the reality of our limitations and weakness as well as the reality that we are so gifted by nature and by grace. It is in learning to face the holistic vision of the weak and wayward as well as the gifted and graced sides of ourselves that we find true happiness.

> The supreme happiness in life
> is in the conviction that we are loved
> not because of what we are
> but in spite of it.
> *(Victor Hugo)*

Jesus makes it clear in the gospels that the main source of our happiness is a vision which he wishes to open up for us by making himself and thus his Father known to us.

> All things have been handed over to me by my Father; and no one knows who the Son is except the Father, or who the Father is except the Son and anyone to whom the Son chooses to reveal him. Then turning to the disciples, Jesus said to them privately, 'Blessed are the eyes that see what you see! For I tell you that many prophets and kings desired to see what you see, but did not see it, and to hear what you hear, but did not hear it.' (Lk 10:23-24)

To maintain this vision, Jesus gives us the Mass in which we remember the story of his love expressed in the events of his passion, death and resurrection. Just as the Passover meal, in which the Mass is set, was meant to help people re-enact the events of the Exodus and thus savour the love of God which inspired them, so in the Mass we tell the story of Jesus' unlimited love for us so that we might be nourished by it. 'Then he took a loaf of bread, and when he had given thanks, he broke it and gave it to them, saying, "This is my body, which is given for you. Do this in remembrance of me." And he did the same with the cup after supper, saying, "This cup that is poured out for you is the new covenant in my blood".' (Lk 22:7-20)

The vision on which our joy depends includes a shadow side of us. Facing this involves becoming aware of our limitations and accepting our human poverty in the way that God accepts and even delights in the prodigal son in us. The dominant sentiment in Luke's description of the way Jesus and the Father respond to this prodigal in each of us is joy.

> And when he comes home, he calls together his friends and neighbours, saying to them, 'Rejoice with me, for I have found my sheep that was lost.' Just so, I tell you, there will be more joy in heaven over one sinner who repents … Quickly, bring out a robe – the best one – and put it on him; put a ring on his finger and sandals on his feet. And get the fatted calf and kill it, and let us eat and celebrate; for this son of mine was dead and is alive again. (Lk 15:6-7, 20-24)

It is hard to maintain this positive vision of ourselves and to prevent the negative one from dominating us, especially when we go through hard times. It is Jesus' wish to sustain and console us in these dark times as he sustained his disciples when he began to prepare them to face the passion and death he knew he must undergo. After he predicts these events he gives his disciples a vision in which they see the terrible events he predicts in their true light. (Lk 9:28-36)

> From tomorrow on I shall be sad. From tomorrow on, not today, today I shall be glad. And every day no matter how bitter it may be I shall say, From tomorrow on I shall be sad – not today. *(Prayer of a child in a Nazi death camp)*

FEATURE 5

'The work of God'

To be truly happy requires a lot of hard work. This is because the depth and permanence of our happiness rests on the conviction that we are loved and developing this conviction involves a radical change of mind and heart. This radical change is required because distorted images of God and of ourselves have become firmly established in us and it takes a prolonged, disciplined effort to dislodge them. But dislodge them we must if we are to make way for the image of ourselves as loved and lovable on which our happiness depends.

In this feature we look at the task we have to undertake if we are to develop the conviction of being loved on which our happiness rests. Jesus describes what we must do as 'abiding in' the love he has for us and this we do by keeping his commandments. At the heart of these is the Great Commandment that we receive his love and return it with our 'whole heart and soul and mind and strength'.

> As the Father has loved me, so I have loved you; abide in my love. If you keep my commandments, you will abide in my love, just as I have kept my Father's commandments and abide in his love. I have said these things to you so that my joy may be in you, and that your joy may be complete. (Jn 15:9-11)

This means that to be truly happy we need to 'abide in' Jesus' love in the sense that we let it permeate our whole person, our senses and feelings, our capacity to pick up intuitive glimpses of our true self and with our capacity to build these glimpses into the convictions in which our faith consists. Learning to relate with Jesus at these different levels of our experience, and thus learning to believe in his love, is very hard work but it is what Jesus calls 'the work of God'. 'This is the work of God, that you believe in him whom he has sent.' (Jn 6:29)

In the parable of the talents, Jesus expresses in symbolic form what we need to do if we are to 'enter the joy of our master'. The parable challenges us to take responsibility for accepting or believing in the gift of God's love that Jesus reveals to us in his own person. We have both to become aware of and to appropriate this love. The alternative is that we bury this gift or leave it lie dormant and the temptation to do this is very real as Jesus makes clear in his parable of the sower.

> Other seed fell on rocky ground, where it did not have much soil, and it sprang up quickly, since it had no depth of soil. And when the sun rose, it was scorched; and since it had no root, it withered away. Other seed fell among thorns, and the thorns grew up and choked it, and it yielded no grain. (Mk 4:1-20)

Jesus never disguises the fact that belief in his love, as the deepest source of our joy, demands a change of mind and heart. (Mk 1:14-15) The work involved in making this change is so difficult that Jesus compares it to dying. Just as the seed must die if is to germinate so we have to die to distorted ways of seeing life if these are to be replaced by what Jesus asks us to believe. (Jn 12:24-25)

From early on in his public life, Jesus makes it clear on several occasions that the road to his resurrection lies through his passion and death. He takes the road to Jerusalem even though he knows that this decision will involve appalling suffering and a shameful death. (Mk 10:32-34) However, he is aware of how profoundly his death will effect his disciples and that it will draw them into his love for them and the joy that belief in this love brings with it. (Jn 12:32)

At the heart of our struggle to share the joy of Jesus is prayer or what has been called 'the combat of dialogue'. This combat is what is involved in taking seriously Jesus' oft-repeated call to listen and 'hold fast to the word with a noble and generous heart'. (Lk 8:15)

> While he was saying this, a woman in the crowd raised her voice and said to him, 'Blessed is the womb that bore you and the breasts that nursed you!' But he said, 'Happy rather are those who hear the word of God and obey it!' (Lk 11:27-28)

FEATURE 6

The joy Jesus finds in reconciliation

There is a special joy experienced when we are reconciled with those from whom we have become estranged. There are a number of ways this reconciliation can come about and each of these has its own distinctive joy. There is a joy for instance in forgiving others and in inviting them to forgive themselves so that they do not hold on to the painful guilt they experience as a result of what they have done. There is a special kind of joy experienced when others identify with us in the wrong we have done and tell us that they too are familiar with the temptation we have succumbed to. There is also a distinctive joy we experience when others put the wrong we have done in perspective and help us to see it as but a small part of who we are for them. Finally, when others humbly reveal their weakness we become aware of the heroism of their struggle and rejoice in this.

When Jesus appears to his disciples after his Resurrection, he is anxious to repair the rift in their relationship with him caused by their desertion of him during his passion. He wants them to be assured of his forgiveness and not to hold on to the guilt they feel as a result of their abandoning him. Knowing that this need for forgiveness will arise again, he leaves them with a means of being reconciled when through sin they become estranged from him. For Jesus the gift of reconciliation is an essential part of sharing the joy or peace of his resurrection with his disciples.

> 'Peace be with you. As the Father has sent me, so I send you.' When he had said this, he breathed on them and said to them, 'Receive the Holy Spirit. If you forgive the sins of any, they are forgiven them; if you retain the sins of any, they are retained.' (Jn 20:19-23)

A striking characteristic of Jesus' life is the obvious enjoyment he gets in being with the outcasts and sinners of his society. He shows this desire to identify with them by defending adamantly the rightness of his sharing a meal with someone like Levi. 'Then Levi gave a great banquet for him in his house; and there was a large crowd of tax collectors and others sitting at the table with them. The Pharisees and their scribes were complaining to his disciples, saying, 'Why do you eat and drink with tax collectors and sinners?' Jesus answered, 'Those who are well have no need of a physician, but those who are sick; I have come to call not the righteous but sinners to repentance.' (Lk 5:27-32) The letter to the Hebrews expresses the belief that Jesus identifies with the sinner in each of us. It says that he is familiar with our weakness and feels it in such a way that he knows our weakness and our temptations from the inside and can therefore empathise with us. (Heb 4:15)

Those with whom Jesus associates in the gospels suffer from that human tendency to focus on what is wrong with others. Jesus, however, tends to highlight people's goodness and not to dwell with their defects. We notice this very positive attitude of Jesus in the way he relates with the woman in Simon's house. The fact that she is a source of embarrassment to Simon and to his guests does not influence Jesus' estimation of her as a basically good person. He has this rare capacity to highlight the 90% of people that is good and to accept in the light of this the 10% that is weak; he is completely at home with this woman who is an embarrassment to everyone else. (Lk 7:44-47)

In spite of the fact that we are 'pitiably poor', Jesus seeks our company and wants to celebrate with a meal the joy he finds in our company. (Rev 3:17, 20-21) In the three parables in Lk 15 Jesus expresses his joy in finding and being reconciled with the areas of people's lives which they have repressed and become estranged from.

> What woman having ten silver coins, if she loses one of them, does not light a lamp, sweep the house, and search carefully until she finds it? When she has found it, she calls together her friends and neighbours, saying, 'Rejoice with me, for I have found the coin that I had lost.' Just so, I tell you, there is joy in the presence of the angels of God over one sinner who repents.' (Lk 15:1-10)

FEATURE 7

Raising us from desolation to consolation

We all have experience of wanting to rescue those we love from the hardships and the painful situations they find themselves in. We also know the joy we experience when we succeed in helping them to rise above their troubles. Helping others in this way demands sensitivity and patience, as people must be allowed to set their own pace in making their way through their valley of darkness. Kübler Ross, in her book *On Death and Dying*, warns us of the danger of urging those who have undergone some traumatic experience to move through the five stages they are likely to pass through more quickly than they are ready to. We must each find the light from within in our own time.

> People are like stained-glass windows. They sparkle and shine when the sun is out, but when the darkness sets in, their true beauty is revealed only if there is a light from within. *(Elizabeth Kübler Ross)*

In this feature we will examine how Jesus, by fostering our faith, especially in times of hardship, transforms our sadness into joy and raises us from desolation to consolation. When Jesus anticipates his return to his Father he realises what a threat this will be to the joy his disciples experience in his resurrection. He is aware of the danger of his disciples interpreting his departure as an abandonment of them and the desolation this might cause. He, therefore, wishes to reassure them that his leaving them will mean the opening up of the possibility of his being with them in a new and deeper way than before. So in the apparent absence of Jesus, when he seems to leave us, there is an invitation to find the joy of his presence in a new way through faith.

> I did not say these things to you from the beginning, because I was with you. But now I am going to him who sent me; yet none of you asks me, 'Where are you going?' But because I have said these things to you, sorrow has filled your hearts. Nevertheless I tell you the truth: it is to your advantage that I go away, for if I do not go away, the Advocate will not come to you; but if I go, I will send him to you. (Jn 16:1-7)

It is obvious from the joy that permeates the Acts of the Apostles that the following prediction of Jesus has come true and that after his ascension his disciples have found him present in a more profound and permanent way than before. This new way he is present brings with it a profound and permanent joy.

> Very truly, I tell you, you will weep and mourn, but the world will rejoice; you will have pain, but your pain will turn into joy. When a woman is in labour, she has pain, because her hour has come. But when her child is born, she no longer remembers the anguish because of the joy of having brought a human being into the world. So you have pain now; but I will see you again, and your hearts will rejoice, and no one will take your joy from you. (Jn 16:19-22, Jn 6:16-21) 'Do not let your hearts be troubled. Believe in God, believe also in me.' (Jn 14:1)

When Jesus meets two desolate disciples on the road to Emmaus we see how he leads the two out of despair and sadness and into enthusiasm and joy. He does this by inviting them to notice and articulate their experience with a view to sharing it with him. It is only after patiently waiting for them to do this that Jesus helps them to interpret their experience in the light of the word and of the 'breaking of the bread'. In this way he leads them step-by-step on an exodus-like journey out of their sadness and despair and into the consolation and joy that faith in his abiding presence brings.

> 'Were not our hearts burning within us while he was talking to us on the road, while he was opening the scriptures to us?' ... Then they told what had happened on the road, and how he had been made known to them in the breaking of the bread. (Lk 24:13-35, Lk 19:1-10)

FEATURE 8

Profound and pervasive joy

It is hard, in the often desolate cultural atmosphere in which we live today, to sustain the belief that we are made for joy, and to let this joy involve us wholly and deeply. The idea that joy consists mainly or even exclusively in the instant and intense pleasure we get from our relationships or from material things is prevalent today. The joy that we contemplate in this feature, however, is a quiet, gradual and lifelong growth that is a healthy mix of a joy that we are meant to draw from all the levels of our experience.

> Joy balances satisfaction of sense and soul
> And mind's conviction felt at heart's core
> A sober inebriation of embodied spirit.

We have been looking at joy as something that has its origins in our experience of being loved and of returning that love. This love and the joy associated with it is experienced, according to the Great Commandment, in four ways, through our 'heart, soul, mind and strength'. These are the kinds of joy we derive from our senses and our feelings, from the glimpses we get of what is true and worthwhile and from the convictions we form from these. It is from a healthy mixture of these four kinds of joy that the complete happiness that Jesus wants for us emerges as a temperate joy that we might term 'sober inebriation'.

Jesus enjoys eating, drinking and talking with those he meets, including outcasts and sinners such as Zacchaeus and Levi. When the Scribes and Pharisees contrast his lifestyle with that of John the Baptist they typify him as a glutton and a drunkard. (Mt 11:18-19) Jesus speaks about joy in a sensate way, in terms of banquets and wedding feasts and also in terms of very simple things such as the wondrous beauty of flowers.

> Consider the lilies, how they grow: they neither toil nor spin; yet I tell you, even Solomon in all his glory was not clothed like one of these. (Lk 12:27)

Jesus' idea of joy is deeply associated with feelings. He speaks of the joy he wishes to share with us as being like that which a mother experiences after the pain of childbirth when she looks at her baby. (Jn 16:21) He experiences sadness that is so deep that it causes him to break down and cry when he witnesses the tragedy of his own people refusing the peace he comes to bring them. (Lk 19:41-42) He is enthusiastic about the prospect of proclaiming the good news (Jn 4:34-38) and expresses his feelings of joy and gratitude that awareness of his Father's goodness arouses in him. (Lk 10:21)

Jesus is highly perceptive of the signs of people's faith and ready to voice his appreciation of this as well as his concern for their peace. (Mk 5:34) By what he says and the miracles he works Jesus is always trying to give people joy in the glimpse he seeks to give them of his Father's love and providence in their lives. (Lk 12:22-32)

What Jesus ultimately aims at in giving us glimpses of his Father's love is that we would listen to these glimpses and that they would thus become the convictions in which faith consists. It is through believing in Jesus' love in this way that our joy becomes 'complete'.

> As the Father has loved me, so I have loved you; abide in my love. If you keep my commandments, you will abide in my love, just as I have kept my Father's commandments and abide in his love. I have said these things to you so that my joy may be in you, and that your joy may be complete. (Jn 15:9-11)

As we observe Jesus in the gospel stories, his joy may not be obvious to us. This may be because we have become accustomed to Jesus being very serious, but it is also due to the fact that his joy is so profound, enduring and pervasive that it is a quiet joy or a sober inebriation. It is a joy that pervades his whole person just as the love that is its source pervades his 'whole heart, soul, mind and strength'. (Lk 10:25-28)

THE EIGHTH PORTRAIT

The passionate love of Jesus

The people who give us a glimpse of the love depicted in this portrait are those who are in love. The *passionate nature of their love* is characterised by its intensity, by the way it involves their whole person and focuses all their attention on their beloved. The passion with which they love leads them to be *magnanimous* in the sense that they would do anything for those they love. Their magnanimity is seen in their passion for truth, for justice and in the energy they put into expressing in action what they are convinced is true and worthwhile.

The truth they are passionate about is not just an intellectual one but more an experience of our true self which they communicate in the way they relate with us. Their *passion for justice* can be seen in the way that those they love become the centre of their concern and they evaluate everything in the light of this love. They experience a deep desire *to live consistently with what they believe* to be true and just so that their lives are characterised by a child-like simplicity, honesty and candour.

There is a *generative* side to those who make this portrait real for us in that they enliven us by the way they accept our weaknesses, appreciate our strengths and in their concern that we accomplish all that we are capable of. Finally, with their passion for truth, justice and integrity they exercise a *transforming power* in our lives as they urge us to establish authentic relationships with God and with ourselves, with others and with all creation.

The features of the eight portrait of Jesus

1. Jesus thinks of himself and each of us as being the beloved of the Father, the one in whom the Father delights. Like John, each of us is *'the beloved disciple'*, the one whom Jesus loves to the utmost extent.

2. The intense or *passionate nature of Jesus' love* for each of us is a reflection of his passionate love for his Father, of the fact that he loves him and us with his whole person, or to the utmost extent.

3. The passion with which Jesus relates makes him *magnanimous* in that it transforms his vision, his values and his lifestyle. It makes him passionate about the truth, about justice and about authentic living.

4. Jesus is *passionate about the truth* or about the revelation of his Father's love that he embodies or personifies. This is 'the good news' we encounter when we contemplate Jesus in a gospel story.

5. The values Jesus is passionate about lead to his *profound sense of justice*. This centres on his commandment that we love others and all creation as he has loved us.

6. Jesus has a passion for living authentically or for *living consistently with his vision and values*, with what he sees to be true and just. Thus the way Jesus acts gives us a sense of energy, power or assertiveness.

7. This power of Jesus is *generative* in that his acceptance of our weakness, his appreciation of our strengths and his concern for our best interests is truly life-giving.

8. This *magnetic power* of Jesus' love draws us to him so forcefully that it not only establishes a healthy relationship with him but with ourselves, with others and with all creation as well.

FEATURE 1
'My beloved in whom I delight'

In this feature we draw on our experience of a love that is variously termed romantic, passionate and being in love. Even though we might have difficulty defining the nature of this love we know what it feels like and how it effects ourselves and others. It can be the most impermanent of loves, but while it lasts, it is the most dramatic in the way it transforms people's lives, the way they think, feel and behave. While we usually think of romantic love as being confined to human beings, it has always been seen as a profound way of understanding the relationship Jesus draws each person into.

In the Old Covenant we are often spoken of as God's beloved, especially in the Song of Songs. Compared to the way this image of our relationship with God is highlighted in the Song, the fact that we are the beloved of Jesus seems to be played down in the gospels. Yet, the fact that we are Jesus' beloved disciples and that he loves us passionately is well founded in the gospels and is central to Christian tradition, as expressed from Origen's time to that of St John of the Cross.

An essential part of understanding our relationship to Jesus as his beloved is that Jesus shares with us his own relationship with the Father. In John's gospel this relationship is built around our coming to 'know' Jesus' love for us, just as he knows his Father's love and his Father knows his. 'I know my own and my own know me, just as the Father knows me and I know the Father.' (Jn 10:14-15). Now, an essential part of sharing their relationship is that we are Jesus' beloved just as he is the Father's beloved. 'As the Father has loved me, so I have loved you; abide in my love.' (Jn 15:9) The fact that the relationship we are being drawn into is one between the lover and his beloved is clear from the baptism of Jesus. There the Father addresses Jesus as his beloved in whom he delights.

> You are my Son, the Beloved; with you I am well pleased. (Lk 3:21-22)

This relationship of Jesus as the beloved of the Father is seen in the gospels as a fulfilment of the prophecy of Isaiah about the coming Messiah. 'Here is my servant, whom I uphold, my chosen, in whom my soul delights.' (Is 42:1)

In a few gospel stories, Jesus explicitly portrays himself as the bridegroom. 'The wedding guests cannot fast while the bridegroom is with them, can they? As long as they have the bridegroom with them, they cannot fast.' (Mk 2:19-20) When Jesus speaks of himself as the bridegroom he is drawing on a long tradition in the Old Testament where we are spoken of as God's beloved (Song 2:10), betrothed (Hos 2:22), bride (Isa 62:5) and wife. (Jer 31:22) Even if all these images are not explicitly used in the gospels, they have become in Christian tradition an essential way of understanding our relationship with Jesus.

From the time of Origen, the early Christian scholar, the Song of Songs became the context in which Christians understand their relationship with Jesus. This way of seeing life was deeply influenced by the parallel which Paul, in his letter to the Ephesians, drew between the intimate relationship of a husband and wife in marriage and that between Christ and the Christian.

> Husbands, love your wives, just as Christ loved the church and gave himself up for her, in order to make her holy by cleansing her with the washing of water by the word, so as to present the church to himself in splendour. (Eph 5:25-27)

Where John sees Mary Magdalene as the beloved of Jesus in the sense that her quest for him pervades her life, he sees himself as the beloved disciple because of his experience of the intensity of Jesus' love for him. Like Paul John sees his life in the light of what for him is the central reality of the gospel which is that Jesus loves him 'to the end', 'to the utmost extent' or 'to death'.

> Having loved his own who were in the world, he loved them to the end. (Jn 13:1) It is no longer I who live, but it is Christ who lives in me. And the life I now live in the flesh I live by faith in the Son of God, who loved me and gave himself for me. (Gal 2:20)

FEATURE 2

Living life with a passion

We may have difficulty envisioning ourselves being engaged in a relationship with Jesus that is passionate. The reason may be that we find it difficult to identify with Jesus as a passionate person, or that we belong to a culture which identifies passion with the physical and sexual side of ourselves. Again, it may be due to an excessively spiritual view of Jesus, which tends to repress much of what we associate with the more passionate side of human nature. In this feature, therefore, we need to focus on some concrete ways of making the passionate relationship Jesus wishes to establish with us more real and more relevant to our experience. To do this we will interpret the passionate love of Jesus for us to mean that we are the centre of his attention, the object of his intense devotion and that his whole person, mind and heart, soul and senses is involved in his relationship with us.

Jesus is passionate about life and about sharing its fullness with us. 'I came that they may have life, and have it abundantly.' (Jn 10:10) He explains what he means by life in terms of a profound and passionate relationship that he uses the word 'know' to express. It is a relationship in which we know the Father, the Spirit and Jesus in the way they know each other. (Jn 10:14-15) When we look for the meaning of the word *know* as Jesus uses it we find that it consists in being given an intimate knowledge of being loved wholly and deeply by the persons of the Trinity. The example that is used, especially by the prophets Hosea and Jeremiah, to illustrate this love is the most intimate human relationship, that between a man and a woman. (Hos 2:14-20)

Making this love of God known to us is the main thrust of Jesus' life and it is a love which is focused on each person, on 'the least no less than the greatest'. (Jer 31:34) This one-to-one relationship is so personal, permanent and profound that Jesus compares it to that which he has with his Father.

> He calls his own sheep by name and leads them out ... I am the good shepherd. I know my own and my own know me, just as the Father knows me and I know the Father. And I lay

down my life for the sheep. (Jn 10:3-15)

Those Jesus loves passionately, as well as being the centre of his attention, are the object of intense devotion. There is no sacrifice Jesus will not make for them. This wholehearted devotion is a characteristic of Jesus that he highlights in his parable of the good shepherd. (Jn 10:11-18) The gospel story emphasises this too, especially when it describes the intensity of Jesus' love manifest in his passion, death and resurrection. 'No one has greater love than this, to lay down one's life for one's friends.' (Jn 15:13) The intensity of Jesus' love for us is captured by the image he uses to describe it when he says that he has come to set the world on fire with his love.

I came to bring fire to the earth, and how I wish it were already kindled! (Lk 12:49)

A very distinctive characteristic of passionate love is that it is so intense that it engages our whole person, body, soul, heart and mind. This is the way Jesus wants us to be passionately engaged by his love when he invites us to 'abide in' it by keeping his commandments. 'As the Father has loved me, so I have loved you; abide in my love. If you keep my commandments, you will abide in my love, just as I have kept my Father's commandments and abide in his love.' (Jn 15:9-10) At the core of these commandments is the call to be loved by Jesus and to love in return with our whole heart and soul, with our whole strength and mind. It is a call to respond to Jesus' passionate love in a passionate way for it is in being loved and in loving in this passionate way that we find life in all its fullness.

'What must I do to inherit eternal life?' He said to him, 'What is written in the law? What do you read there?' He answered, 'You shall love the Lord your God with all your heart, and with all your soul, and with all your strength, and with all your mind; and your neighbour as yourself.' And he said to him, 'You have given the right answer; do this, and you will live.' (Lk 10:25-27)

157

FEATURE 3

'A noble and generous heart'

The people who love us with a passion are rarely small-minded or preoccupied with what is petty. They concern themselves with major issues, with a broad vision of life and respond to us in a wholehearted or generous way. Nevertheless, there is a strong tendency in human nature to reduce the broad vision and the basic values to what is practical and then to become exclusively concerned with these common sense practicalities. By contrast, the people who give us our strongest impression of this feature are magnanimous and generous and they show this in the way they devote themselves wholeheartedly to what they consider to be priorities. We recognise the magnanimity of people also in the way they act in that they single out the more important things that need doing and do these energetically.

Throughout the gospels Jesus retains a magnanimity of spirit that springs from his devotion to making known his Father's love and providence to us. (Jn 17:26) This largeness of spirit effects the way he thinks, the values he lives by and the way he acts. He contrasts the pettiness of the rules that the Scribes and Pharisees have drawn up with the basic issues of compassion and justice he feels passionately about.

> While he was speaking, a Pharisee invited him to dine with him; so he went in and took his place at the table. The Pharisee was amazed to see that he did not first wash before dinner ... 'For you tithe mint and rue and herbs of all kinds, and neglect justice and the love of God; it is these you ought to have practised, without neglecting the others.' (Lk 11:37-42)

As we see from this incident, Jesus always focuses on the real issues of life and death. He centres his attention on 'the one thing necessary' and on what in the light of this are people's real needs. He challenges us as he did Martha not to allow ourselves to be distracted from pursuing these.

> But the Lord answered her, 'Martha, Martha, you are worried and distracted by many things; there is need of only one thing. Mary has chosen the better part, which will not be taken away from her.' (Lk 10:41-42)

In his parables about the treasure hidden in the field and the pearl of great price Jesus stresses this necessity of keeping our minds and hearts focused on what is central.

> The kingdom of heaven is like treasure hidden in a field, which someone found and hid; then in his joy he goes and sells all that he has and buys that field. Again, the kingdom of heaven is like a merchant in search of fine pearls; on finding one pearl of great value, he went and sold all that he had and bought it. (Mt 13:44-48)

Jesus demonstrates how these two parables are lived out in his own life by the way he focused all his energies on bringing us life through his passion and death. What preoccupies him, therefore, throughout his public life is his journey to Jerusalem. There he brings to a dramatic conclusion his work of giving us the fullness of life or what he calls 'eternal life'.

> For God so loved the world that he gave his only Son, so that everyone who believes in him may not perish but may have eternal life. (Jn 3:14-16)

It is in the giving of his life for us and being among us as one who serves that Jesus finds true greatness and that we see the true magnanimity of Jesus. It is in being at our service in this way that he empowers us to love others as he loves us, to be magnanimous like he is.

> A dispute also arose among them as to which one of them was to be regarded as the greatest. But he said to them, 'The kings of the Gentiles lord it over them; and those in authority over them are called benefactors. But not so with you; rather the greatest among you must become like the youngest, and the leader like one who serves. … I am among you as one who serves.' (Lk 22:24-30)

FEATURE 4

A passion for the truth

The people who make this feature real for us have a passion for the truth. They have a strong desire to be true to the light, to be genuine, authentic and honest; they are quick to detect hypocrisy or a lack of integrity. They tend to challenge us to walk in the light and confront us when they find double standards in the way we think and live. But the truth they are passionate about is not just intellectual integrity because for them what is true and real centres on their relationships. In these they experience the truth as a vision of themselves seen in the eyes of others who accept and affirm them. They in turn give us a sense of our true self with their capacity for acceptance, appreciation and concern. They challenge us to become aware of and to believe in all we have become and in all we may become. The truth discovered in their relationships is very real and moving for them.

Jesus sees the truth as the revelation of God's love and providence that he makes to us in his own person. Since Jesus identifies with this truth we come to know it in coming to know him. 'Jesus said to him, "I am the way, and the truth, and the life. No one comes to the Father except through me".' (Jn 14:6) Jesus is the truth in the sense that by becoming a human being he reveals the Father's love – the way he accepts and affirms us – in terms that are visible, audible and tangible. 'And the Word became flesh and lived among us, and we have seen his glory, the glory as of a father's only son, full of grace and truth.' (Jn 1:14)

Jesus' whole life centres on making the truth known to us and so he begins and concludes his public life with a statement of this his main intent.

> No one has ever seen God. It is God the only Son, who is close to the Father's heart, who has made him known. (Jn 1:18) ... I made your name known to them, and I will make it known, so that the love with which you have loved me may be in them, and I in them. (Jn 17:26)

One of the qualities that characterise this feature of Jesus' passion for the truth is that he is attuned to what each person he meets is ready to hear. He adapts the truth to each person, so that his approach to Nicodemus in chapter three of John's gospel is very different from the way he approaches the Samaritan woman in chapter four. He challenges each with belief in the truth he proclaims and with the radical change of mind and heart that belief always involves.

Throughout the gospels Jesus urges people to believe the truth he reveals about his love for them and therefore about their lovableness in his eyes. There are a variety of reasons we may fail to believe in or accept this truth but the most common one is the distorted images of Jesus and of ourselves that we have adopted. These distorted images block belief in the true image of ourselves which Jesus reflects back to us as we come to know him and who we are in his eyes. Changing these images is what Jesus calls repentance, the change of mind and heart that is necessary if we are to believe the good news. 'The kingdom is at hand, repent, and believe in the good news.' (Mk 1:14-15) Jesus confronts us with the radical nature of this change and with the tragedy of not accepting all that is involved in undergoing it.

> Those who believe in him are not condemned; but those who do not believe are condemned already, because they have not believed in the name of the only Son of God. (Jn 3:17-21)

The tragedy of the varying degrees of our unbelief is a major theme in John's gospel. It is expressed initially in the prologue and then illustrated, for example, by the Pharisees in the story of the man born blind (Jn 9:1-41) and in the story of Pilate. (Jn 18:28-40) The tragedy of these people is that they meet Jesus but refuse to listen to him and so remain with their deadening illusions about him and about themselves.

> He was in the world, and the world came into being through him; yet the world did not know him. He came to what was his own, and his own people did not accept him. But to all who received him … he gave power to become children of God. (Jn 1:9-12)

FEATURE 5

A passion for justice

People who give us an impression of this feature have a strong sense of what is just and unjust and of when the way someone is being treated is fair or unfair. This feeling for what is just or fair comes from a judgment they make as to whether what is happening is consistent with the way they value themselves and others. Their way of valuing everything is determined by what they make the centre of their concern, for the relative value of everything else is determined by this. For example, if we make wealth, and the power it brings with it, the main thing we set our hearts on, then our relationships will become secondary to this. We will as a result be unjust to ourselves and to others in the sense that we do not give these relationships the importance they are due. It is of the nature of passionate love to make relationships and the love that is at the core of them central.

For Jesus what is central to justice springs from what he sees to be the truth, or 'the one thing necessary'. This is expressed in his commandment that we love others as he loves us. The relative importance or value of everything is judged in the light of this. We must first of all abide or believe in Jesus' love and then evaluate everything with this in mind.

> As the Father has loved me, so I have loved you; abide in my love. If you keep my commandments, you will abide in my love, just as I have kept my Father's commandments and abide in his love. (Jn 15:9-10)

On the basis of this experience of our true value in Jesus' eyes we get an intimate knowledge of what is the true value of people and of all creation. Jesus invites us to love others in the way that he loves us.

> This is my commandment, that you love one another as I have loved you. No one has greater love than this, to lay down one's life for one's friends. You are my friends if you do what I command you. I do not call you servants any longer, because the servant does not know what the master is doing; but I have called you friends, because I have made

known to you everything that I have heard from my Father. (Jn 15:12-15)

Justice for Jesus consists in giving to God, to ourselves, to others and to the whole of God's creation the love that is their due. Justice also challenges us to discern which ways of behaving are consistent with his love or with the truth or light Jesus brings into the world. (Jn 8:12)

I am the light of the world. Whoever follows me will never walk in darkness but will have the light of life. (John 12:35)

We have a practical example of the way Jesus holds we should treat others justly or fairly in his parable of the Good Samaritan. (Lk 10:25-37)

He gives us an example of what he is saying in this parable in the way he treats two of his disciples on the road to Emmaus. He is sensitive and listens to them rather than passing them by on the other side of the road. He respects where they are in the way, gives them the opportunity to express this, and listens while they do so. He accepts their human limitations and their loss of faith in him. He is like the good Samaritan in the practical concern he shows as he painstakingly leads them out of their despair and into a new sense of faith and hope in his love for them. (Lk 24:13-35)

In his parable of the judgement, Jesus gives us a picture of what he considers to be just or fair and the kinds of behaviour which are consistent with his commandment that we love others as he loves us. 'Truly I tell you, just as you did it to one of the least of these who are members of my family, you did it to me.' (Mt 25:41-46) Jesus' passion for justice leads him to confront the Pharisees with their 'neglect of justice and the love of God'.

But woe to you Pharisees! For you tithe mint and rue and herbs of all kinds, and neglect justice and the love of God; it is these you ought to have practised, without neglecting the others. (Lk 11:42-44)

FEATURE 6

'Power came out from him'

We get an impression of this feature from our experience of the power, energy and passion with which certain people relate with us. This power is seen in the active way they pursue truth and justice and what they feel they should do to live consistently with what they know to be true and of value. The magnanimity of those who love passionately ultimately finds expression in the energy and assertiveness with which they express their love in action. Besides the way they feel challenged in their own lives to act consistently with what they are convinced is true and worthwhile, they take up other people's causes and fight them in a forceful or assertive way. When they are on our side we are left in no doubt as to where they stand and where we stand in their estimation. They show this by the forceful way they act on our behalf for they believe that love is shown more by deeds than by words.

In this feature we look at the passion, the energy and the assertive way Jesus pursues what he sees to be the truth and what is just. He does this by word and by deed. He speaks and acts 'with authority and power'.

> They were all amazed and kept saying to one another, 'What kind of utterance is this? For with authority and power he commands the unclean spirits, and out they come!' (Lk 4:36)

Jesus goes about the revelation of himself to us through what he does as well as through what he says. He reveals himself to us through what the gospels call 'deeds of power'.

> On the Sabbath he began to teach in the synagogue, and many who heard him were astounded. They said, 'Where did this man get all this? What is this wisdom that has been given to him? What deeds of power are being done by his hands! (Mk 6:2)

These 'deeds of power' are a reference to the miracles Jesus did and they correspond to the 'wonderful works' God did during the Exodus. Like these 'wonderful works' the miracles are signs of the power of Jesus manifesting his passionate concern for us.

Did I not tell you that if you believed, you would see the glory of God? (Jn 11:40)

The power of Jesus is manifest in three kinds of miracles by which he heals people, sets them free and raises them to life.. These occupy a large part of a typical day in the life of Jesus such as that described in the first three chapters of Mark's gospel. (Mk 1:21-3:6). There we see a picture of a dynamic Jesus setting out on his public ministry to proclaim good news in his words as well as in his 'deeds of power'.

> The Spirit of the Lord is upon me, because he has anointed me to bring good news to the poor. He has sent me to proclaim release to the captives and recovery of sight to the blind, to let the oppressed go free. (Lk 4:18)

The power of Jesus is revealed when he heals the woman who suffered from haemorrhages. To understand what is happening in this incident it is important to advert to the fact that the deepest level of healing takes place through our faith in the love of Jesus, of which the miracle is a sign. (Mk 5:24-34)

The miracles are also a manifestation of the power of Jesus to set people free from what oppresses them. When Jesus calms the storm he manifests his power over nature but more profoundly he reveals his power to set people free from the paralysing influence of fear. (Jn 6:16-21) A third kind of miracle reveals the power of Jesus to give us life. One of these miracles, the raising of Lazarus from the dead, focuses our attention on Jesus' desire to use his power to give us life through the faith which he hopes the miracle will inspire.

> For your sake I am glad I was not there, so that you may believe ... I am the resurrection and the life. Those who believe in me, even though they die, will live, and everyone who lives and believes in me will never die. Do you believe this? (Jn 11:15, 25-26)

FEATURE 7

The generative quality of Jesus' life

Generative people are those who by their respect, acceptance, appreciation and concern give us life and help us to sustain it. Even though their concern is assertive and challenging it is not abrasive, as they are well tuned in to and respect where we are. They know when and how to urge us to be true to the light and to act consistently with it. They sense the truth we are ready to face at any particular time in our life and know the right amount of pressure to put on us to live consistently with that truth. The pressure they exert is generative in that it is sensitive to what we are ready for and how we should move towards this.

The generative quality of Jesus appears especially in the way he accepts human weakness, appreciates the good people have done and is concerned to foster their faltering efforts to be better. Matthew draws our attention to the tolerant and gentle way that Jesus encourages growth in people and he sees this as a fulfilment of the prophecy of Isaiah that the Messiah would 'not break a bruised reed or quench a smouldering wick'.

'Here is my servant, whom I have chosen, my beloved, with whom my soul is well pleased. I will put my Spirit upon him, and he will proclaim justice to the Gentiles. He will not wrangle or cry aloud, nor will anyone hear his voice in the streets. He will not break a bruised reed or quench a smouldering wick until he brings justice to victory. And in his name the Gentiles will hope.' (Mt 12:15-21)

In fulfilment of this prophecy, Jesus takes up the cause of those who are weak or those whom society thinks of as failures. He calls these people 'the little ones' and likens their lack of status to that of children. Jesus finds in these 'little ones' a greatness that their lowly status in society tends to obscure.

At that time the disciples came to Jesus and asked, 'Who is the greatest in the kingdom of heaven?' He called a child, whom he put among them, and said, 'Truly I tell you, unless you change and become like children, you will never enter the kingdom of heaven. Whoever becomes humble like this child is the greatest in the kingdom of heaven. (Mt 18:1-4)

Jesus is sensitive to the presence of children and to all those small people in society they symbolise. He always has time for children and is gentle in the way he deals with them as well as being tireless in pursuing their best interests. (Lk 18:15-17)

We see the generative quality of Jesus' acceptance of people in the story of Zacchaeus. He is a corrupt tax-collector who is, as a result, treated as an outcast. Jesus, however, not only accepts Zacchaeus but makes him the centre of attention and highlights the fact that he is as much a son of Abraham, as much a part of the chosen people, as anyone else in the crowd that surrounds Jesus. From Luke's description of this incident we can see how Jesus' acceptance and appreciation of Zacchaeus is so enlivening. (Lk 19:8-10)

We notice the enthusiasm Jesus generates in people like the Samaritan woman. He helps her to gradually discover and appreciate what he calls 'the gift of God' which is the deepest source of her greatness.

> If you knew the gift of God, and who it is that is saying to you, 'Give me a drink', you would have asked him, and he would have given you living water. (Jn 4:10)

She is led to an appreciation of this 'gift' of the love of God in Jesus' down-to-earth acceptance, appreciation and concern for her. We can see how generative this proves to be in the enthusiasm it generates, causing her in turn to become generative.

> Then the woman left her water jar and went back to the city. She said to the people, 'Come and see a man who told me everything I have ever done! He cannot be the Messiah, can he?' They left the city and were on their way to him. (Jn 4:28-30)

FEATURE 8

'I will draw all things to myself'

Some people have a powerful influence on our lives. They manifest this power not so much by challenging and confronting us
as by winning our hearts in an enticing way. They draw us not
just to themselves but to the truth, goodness and beauty they are
devoted to. Where we are inclined to get scattered when we devote ourselves to urgent matters, they put us in touch with what
is important and central to life and infect us with their own enthusiasm to build our lives around what is important.

There is a sequence of miracles running through John's gospel,
starting with that at the wedding feast at Cana and reaching a
climax in the resurrection of Jesus. In this sequence of miracles
there is a mounting sense of Jesus' passionate concern for us, for
our most ordinary needs, which he wishes to meet at Cana, to
our most profound ones which he wishes to meet by 'loving us
to the end'. (Jn 13:1) Because the love revealed by these signs has
a radiance, a beauty or what John calls *glory* innate to it, this exercises a magnetic power over those who believe in this revelation of Jesus' love and are captivated by its beauty.

> Jesus did this, the first of his signs, in Cana of Galilee, and re-
> vealed his glory; and his disciples believed in him. (Jn 2:11)

> And I, when I am lifted up from the earth, will draw all peo-
> ple to myself. (Jn 12:32)

In chapters 3-12 of the book of Genesis we see how the basic relationships of life disintegrate when people separate themselves
from God. It is in this context that John sees the magnetic power
of Jesus bringing together again all those people who had been
scattered by the sinfulness which is symbolised for us in the
story of the Fall. Jesus gathers 'into one the dispersed children of
God.' (Jn 11:49-52)

Because Jesus exercises such power over people's hearts
through the events of his passion and death, John portrays him
as a universal king.

> Pilate asked him, 'So you are a king?' Jesus answered, 'You

say that I am a king. For this I was born, and for this I came into the world, to testify to the truth. Everyone who belongs to the truth listens to my voice.'(Jn 18:37)

John begins his description of the events of the passion, death and resurrection with Jesus' entry into Jerusalem. He sees this as a fulfilment of what the prophet Zechariah says about the entry of the messiah-king into Jerusalem. (Zec 9:9-10, Jn 12:12-15) In this scene what distinguishes Jesus as a king is his gentleness and humility, for even though he is our 'master and Lord' he is among us as one who serves.

> After he had washed their feet, had put on his robe, and had returned to the table, he said to them, 'Do you know what I have done to you? You call me Teacher and Lord – and you are right, for that is what I am. So if I, your Lord and Teacher, have washed your feet, you also ought to wash one another's feet. For I have set you an example, that you also should do as I have done to you.' (Jn 13:12-15)

The powerful attraction of this humble and gentle love exercises a compelling influence on people right from the beginning of the gospels. Luke in particular notes how, within a short time of their meeting him, his disciples 'leave everything' to be with him.

> When they had brought their boats to shore, they left everything and followed him ... After this he went out and saw a tax collector named Levi, sitting at the tax booth; and he said to him, 'Follow me.' And he got up, left everything, and followed him. (Lk 5:11, 27-28)

The price the apostles and successive generations of disciples are willing to pay to be with Jesus is compared by him to carrying his cross.

> Then he said to them all, 'If any want to become my followers, let them deny themselves and take up their cross daily and follow me.' (Lk 9:23)

Jesus does not hide the demands of being with him but urges us to count the cost before we commit ourselves to such a lifelong endeavour. (Lk 14:27)

THE NINTH PORTRAIT

The friendship of Jesus

The people who give us a glimpse of this portrait are our friends. The depth of our relationships with them is based on what we share and this can range from some hobby we have an interest in to a gift of ourselves which we give by revealing ourselves to each other. Underlying whatever friends share is a sense of our being chosen by them and being trusted with some degree of self-revelation which they make to us. In this self-revelation friends trust that their weaknesses will be accepted and their strengths will be appreciated. Basic to friendship is this mutual acceptance of limitations so that these are not allowed to get in the way of our appreciation of the essential goodness we find in each other. Thus friends affirm us by not only appreciating all that we have already achieved but by being concerned that we realise all the potential for life and happiness that we are capable of.

People who make this portrait real for us seek to establish and maintain the friendship they initiate with us. They do this by their ongoing efforts to make themselves known to us and in their effort to come to know the self they each wish to share. The response our friends ask of us is that we would receive the gift of themselves which they offer us and that we would accept and affirm the person they reveal to us just as they offer to do the same with the self we reveal to them. They seek to maintain the friendship they have established with us by regular communication. This requires that they listen and respond honestly to what they each reveal of themselves in an ongoing way. By this mutual sharing they call each other into the intimate relationship of friendship.

The features of this portrait of Jesus

1. The friendship Jesus wishes to establish with us is based on his desire to share with us 'everything' he has and is, his inmost life with his Father. Thus he spends his life making his Father known to us.

2. Jesus wishes to befriend all those areas of us which have become estranged from him. In his effort to do this he forgives our sins, identifies with us in our weakness and puts our sins in perspective.

3. Having surmounted the obstacle our sins can be to friendship, Jesus seeks to build up a friendship with us through affirming us and through acknowledging how important we are for him.

4. By making himself known to us in all he says and does, Jesus constantly seeks to extend and deepen his friendship with us by sharing completely the love and relationship he has with his Father.

5. For our part, entry into friendship with Jesus involves our becoming ever more sensitive and responsive to the ways he makes himself known to us. We listen to his word and make our own of it.

6. In practice, coming to know Jesus and thus sharing in the love and relationship he has with his Father, means making space to get engaged in an ongoing conversation with him.

7. This conversation, called prayer, creates a bond or a union that will be as good as our ability to listen and respond to Jesus' love; it is this love that creates and sustains a friendship that is proportionate to it.

FEATURE 1

One going around making friends

Whatever people share as the basis of their friendship, whether it be something superficial or something profound, there is always a degree of self-revelation involved. In some measure, they give a gift of themselves to each other in self-disclosure. Underlying whatever is shared, whether it be a game they play together or a meal over which they talk about what is happening in their lives, there is an experience of being chosen, of making themselves known to each other and of the trust involved in putting themselves in each other's hands like this. When we reveal ourselves to our friends we trust in their ability to accept our limitations, to appreciate our strengths and to be concerned for us.

> Friendship emerges when two or more discover a common interest, insight or taste. It is when the deer was seen as beautiful as well as edible, and this was articulated and shared, that art and friendship was born in a shared vision. (C. S. Lewis, Four Loves)

We could describe the work of Jesus in the gospels as that of one going around making friends with those he meets and leading them into his own relationship with his Father. When Jesus describes the friendship he wants with us, he says that it is based on sharing with us an intimate knowledge of the love that forms the basis of his relationship with his Father.

> I have called you friends, because I have made known to you everything that I have heard from my Father. (Jn 15:15)

This intimate knowledge Jesus shares with us is the fulfilment of the new covenant announced by the prophet Jeremiah: 'No longer shall they teach one another, or say to each other, "Know the Lord," for they shall all know me, from the least of them to the greatest, says the Lord.' (Jer 31:34)

Revealing this intimate knowledge of his Father's love, which is the basis of the friendship Jesus wishes to establish with us, is the purpose of the Incarnation and of all Jesus says and does in the gospels. Luke hears Jesus declaring that his mission from the

Father is to reveal this interior knowledge of his Father's love, which he calls the 'good news', and to dispose people to listen to it by healing and liberating them. (Lk 4:18)

As Lazarus is presented to us in John's gospel as a friend of Jesus, he is a symbol of the relationship into which Jesus wants to draw each of us.

> Lord, your friend is very ill ... Now Jesus loved Martha and her sister and Lazarus. ... Our friend Lazarus is fallen asleep. (Jn 11:3, 5, 11)

In the gospels we see Jesus going around making friends with people like the family at Bethany and his disciples. 'I tell you, my friends, do not fear those who kill the body, and after that can do nothing more.' (Lk 12:4)

Jesus also draws into his friendship 'the least no less than the greatest', those his contemporaries thought of as sinners and outcasts. As he did with Levi the tax collector, Jesus often initiated this friendship by sharing a meal. The significance of the intimate relationship that this 'table fellowship' sets up was not lost on those Scribes and Pharisees who criticised Jesus for befriending those they considered the outcasts of society. (Lk 5:27-32)

It is in the context of the Mass that Jesus explains to his disciples the deepest significance of the table fellowship he shares with them. This is because it is in the Mass that we keep alive the supreme expression of the love of Jesus for us and it is this love that creates and sustains our friendship with him. This love and the union or fellowship it draws us into is what Jesus refers to when he says that he calls us his friends because he shares with us 'everything' about his own relationship with his Father.

> No one has greater love than this, to lay down one's life for one's friends. ... I do not call you servants any longer, because the servant does not know what the master is doing; but I have called you friends, because I have made known to you everything that I have heard from my Father. (Jn 15:12-15)

FEATURE 2

Befriending the estranged

For people to be friends it is important that they learn to accept one another. We are all a blend of good and bad, of what is ideal and what is less than ideal. Friends highlight what is good about us and in that context accept what is deficient. They do not get so caught up in our weaknesses that they do not accept us as largely good.

> A friend is one to whom one may pour out all the contents of one's heart, chaff and grain together, knowing that the gentlest of hands will take and sift it, keep what is worth keeping and with a breath of kindness blow the rest away. *(Arabian Proverb)*

The acceptance that is essential to friendship can take various forms. Those who accept us forgive the wrong we have done and want us to forgive ourselves. They do not see themselves as being above doing the wrong we have done and so identify with us in our weakness. Friends also see our weakness in perspective, finding us predominantly good and they take delight in the reconciliation that their acceptance of our waywardness brings with it.

The work of Jesus in the gospel can be seen as that of befriending those who have estranged themselves from him or as reconciling all things to himself.

> Through him God was pleased to reconcile to himself all things, whether on earth or in heaven, by making peace. (Col 1:20)

Matthew sees the attitude of Jesus to a sinful world as a fulfilment of the prophecy of Isaiah about the Messiah. 'He will not wrangle or cry aloud, nor will anyone hear his voice in the streets. He will not break a bruised reed or quench a smouldering wick until he brings justice to victory.' (Mt 12:19-20) As a friend Jesus' attitude to us as sinners is gentle, enduring, deferential. In general it is an attitude of acceptance that finds expression in his forgiveness, in his being at home with our weakness, in his desire to put our weakness in perspective and in the joy he finds in being reconciled with us.

In the way Jesus deals with Judas' betrayal we see how true he is to his own teaching about forgiveness and how much he wants to befriend anyone who has become estranged from him. He does not expose Judas to the anger of his fellow disciples by letting them know what Judas is about to do.

> So when he had dipped the piece of bread, he gave it to Judas son of Simon Iscariot ... Jesus said to him, 'Do quickly what you are going to do.' Now no one at the table knew why he said this to him. (Jn 13:26-28)

In his efforts to accept the wayward side of us Jesus is willing not only to forgive us and to invite us to forgive ourselves but he even identifies with us in our human weaknesses and temptations. We are told in the letter to the Hebrews that 'he is familiar with all our weakness and has been tempted in every way that we are'. (Heb 4:14-15) Jesus' desire to identify with our sinful humanity is a part of what is symbolised by his baptism and temptation. (Mk 1:9-13)

Because Jesus has drawn us into his own relationship with his Father the words spoken to him at his baptism are spoken to us as well. Jesus wants us to face this reality and to see our sinfulness in this perspective. He wants us to appreciate the fact that in spite of our weakness each of us remains the beloved in whom the Father delights.

> And when Jesus had been baptised, just as he came up from the water, suddenly the heavens were opened to him and he saw the Spirit of God descending like a dove and alighting on him. And a voice from heaven said, 'This is my Son, the Beloved, with whom I am well pleased.' (Mt 3:16-17)

Jesus invites us to see our sinfulness against the background of the glory he shares with us when he says that we are as lovable in the Father's eyes as he is.

> The glory that you have given me I have given them, so that they may be one, as we are one, that the world may know that you have loved them even as you have loved me. (Jn 1722-23)

FEATURE 3

One who affirms and acknowledges us

Friends not only accept but affirm and acknowledge us as well. This affirmation is at the heart of friendship and it means that our friends appreciate all the good there is in us and are concerned about all the good or the happiness that might yet be ours. They want us to be aware of and to accept the good opinion that they and others have of us. Being acknowledged by our friends means that they are sensitive to and respect us as persons as opposed to being unaware and indifferent to us. Our friends are people for whom we are important so that they say to us in effect, 'It is good that you are.' When we walk into a crowded room where we are aware a friend is present we know that for that person we will be the centre of attention. It is as if by acknowledging us they move us from the periphery of the crowd to its centre.

To those willing to listen to him Jesus proclaims the good news in all he says and does. Essential to this good news is the reality that in the Father's eyes we are as lovable as Jesus is. 'You have loved them even as you have loved me.' (Jn 17:23) Because of the difficulty we have in believing this, Jesus is deeply appreciative of our efforts to do so. We see this appreciation, for example, in the incident where he is deeply moved by the faith of a Roman centurion.

> Truly I tell you, in no one in Israel have I found such faith. (Mt 8:10-11, Mt 9:22, Lk 7:44-47)

As a friend, Jesus affirms us in the sense that he appreciates the goodness which is ours through faith in his love and is deeply concerned that we realise all the possibilities that this faith opens up before us. In the parable of the good Samaritan, Jesus paints a picture of how practical is his concern for us. It is a concern that is sensitive to our need and very practical in its efforts to meet these needs. (Lk 10:33-35) Where the parable of the good Samaritan is a graphic description of the practical nature of Jesus' concern for us, the parable of the good shepherd describes the extent and depth of this concern. Its extent is seen in the range of our needs he attends to, from the more material ones to the abundance of life he wants for us. The depth of his concern appears in the price he is willing to pay that we might have this life.

> I am the good shepherd. I know my own and my own know me, just as the Father knows me and I know the Father. And I lay down my life for the sheep. (Jn 10:10-15)

Jesus is sensitive to and respectful of everyone that he meets. We have two striking examples of this capacity of Jesus to acknowledge people, in the way he called Peter and in the tribute he pays to John the Baptist. When Jesus first calls Peter he takes him out fishing where they can be alone together. He calls him in circumstances where Peter, as a fisherman, would be at home and he works a miracle to highlight the nature and the importance of Peter's call. Peter must have felt deeply honoured for the rest of his life when he remembered the circumstances of his call and how profoundly he was moved by being acknowledged in this way. We can see the profound effect this had on him from the way that he left everything, in order to be with Jesus.

> But when Simon Peter saw it, he fell down at Jesus' knees, saying, 'Go away from me, Lord, for I am a sinful man!' Then Jesus said to Simon, 'Do not be afraid; from now on you will be catching people' … When they had brought their boats to shore, they left everything and followed him. (Lk 5:1-12)

Another person Jesus acknowledges in a striking way is John the Baptist when he declares him to be the greatest of the prophets. Jesus then goes on to acknowledge in a profound way the true greatness of anyone who becomes his follower when he says that 'the least in the kingdom of God is greater than John the Baptist'.

> This is the one about whom it is written, 'See, I am sending my messenger ahead of you, who will prepare your way before you.' Truly I tell you, among those born of women no one has arisen greater than John the Baptist; yet the least in the kingdom of heaven is greater than he. (Mt 11:7-11)

FEATURE 4

'I have called you friends'

Friendship involves taking initiatives not just at its beginning but in an on-going way as the horizons of our sensitivity to and concern for our friends are extended. At the beginning of a friendship, any self revelation is usually unintentional or indirect but as the friendship deepens we are called to share ourselves more directly with another. The decision to do this calls for courage for if we are to make ourselves known at any depth we have to get to know ourselves first. In other words, if we are to answer the call of adult life to become intimate, or to make our inner self known to others, we must first answer the call to discover our identity, or to know our inner self. This involves a lot of hard work but what makes this worthwhile is the experience of joy when that which we share of ourselves is accepted and affirmed.

We have already seen how Jesus goes around making friends, leading those who respond to his initiative into his own relationship with the Father. In this feature we will look at how Jesus, by revealing himself to each person, initiates this friendship and constantly seeks to expand and deepen it by taking fresh initiatives.

Jesus calls us into a friendship with him by inviting us to come to know him and his love for each of us. This is the true significance of Jesus' invitation when he said to his first disciples, 'Come and see!' (Jn 1:35-39) Jesus invites us to come to know him through what he says and what he does, through his word and the works he does. The greatest of these works and the one that reveals the full extent and depth of Jesus' love is his passion, death and resurrection.

> No one has greater love than this, to lay down one's life for one's friends. (John 15:13) We know love by this, that he laid down his life for us. (1 Jn 3:16-18)

In between the initial call of his disciples to be with him and the call to be his friends at the end of his life there is an on-going one to expand and deepen this relationship. This on-going initiative

Contemplating the Word of God

*The most important fact in all of Theology and Spirituality
is that the three persons of the Trinity want
to reveal themselves to each person.*
Karl Rahner

The following way of praying with the word of God assumes that the
Bible is the story of the Trinity's passionate desire to reveal themselves
to you. Each part of this story will reveal some aspect of the Father's
love that Jesus makes visible and that the Spirit gives you an intimate
knowledge of. You can use the following steps to converse with God in
a psalm, for example, or with Jesus in a gospel story.

1 Quieten yourself in whatever way you wish, such as by listening to
   the sounds you hear around you. Then focus your attention on God's
   presence by repeating a word or phrase that helps you to do this.

2 Read a piece of God's word and notice what aspect of God's love it
   reveals to you. Choose a word or a phrase to express and savour this
   love.

3 Spend time letting the attractiveness of this aspect of God's love
   grow. It may help to ponder the way someone you know radiates this
   kind of love.

4 Put words on what, in effect, God is saying in this piece of scripture
   and then let Him say this to you. The more challenging and
   personal the words you choose are the better. Let God say these words
   to you a number of times so that the love they express may sink in.

5 Tell God how you feel about what He says to you. You may find that
   one part of you resists this while another part welcomes it with
   gratitude, hope or joy.

Reflecting on your prayer

If you accept the Gospel and become Christ's, you will stumble on
wonder upon wonder, and every wonder true.
Brendan to King Brude

The purpose of reflection is to become aware of the fact that the Father,
Jesus and their Spirit reveal themselves to you in prayer. It is also meant
to help you to become familiar with how they want to do this by means
of the Spirit enlightening your mind and attracting your heart.
Therefore, when you reflect on your prayer, dwell with the reality that it
is the Spirit who leads you into an intimate knowledge of God's love.
Then, notice and record, however briefly, anything that struck you
about this love during the prayer such as :

- what aspect of God's love you stayed with;

- what you found attractive about this love;

- what words God used to express this love to you;

- how you felt about what He says to you.

Begin your next period of prayer by reading what you have written. This
will give continuity and lead to a build-up of what is being revealed
about God's love to you. From this a true vision of who God is for you
and who you are for God will take shape. In this way you will be
answering Jesus' call to repent and believe the gospel of his Father's
love for you. (Mk 1:15)

Let us hang upon the lips of the faithful
for the Spirit of God is upon every one of them.
Paulinus of Nola

to develop his friendship with us takes the form of a constant effort to make himself known.

> I made your name known to them, and I will make it known, so that the love with which you have loved me may be in them, and I in them. (Jn 17:26)

When Jesus says that he will continue to make the Father's love known to us he is speaking about the Spirit's role of leading us into the full extent and depth of Jesus' love for us.

> I still have many things to say to you, but you cannot bear them now. When the Spirit of truth comes, he will guide you into all the truth; for he will not speak on his own, but will speak whatever he hears, and he will declare to you the things that are to come. (Jn 16:12-13)

In chapter 9 of John's gospel, Jesus develops a relationship with the man born blind as he gradually reveals his love for him according as the man is ready to grasp it. From the way Jesus accepts and affirms and acknowledges him, the man is given a new way of seeing Jesus and of seeing himself in Jesus' eyes. Even though he is rejected by the scribes and Pharisees Jesus accepts him and opens up for him a whole new way of seeing and appreciating himself. Jesus also shows his deep concern for the man who was born blind by leading him step by step into a deeper relationship. We can see the various stages this relationship passes through in its development into a friendship from the sequence of ever more intimate names the man uses for Jesus. The eyes of the man born blind are gradually opened as he is gradually led to realise who Jesus is for him and who he is in the eyes of Jesus.

> I believe he is a prophet. ... if he did not come from God, could he do such a thing? ... Do you believe in the Son of Man? He answered, 'And who is he, sir? Tell me, so that I may believe in him.' Jesus said to him, 'You have seen him, and the one speaking with you is he.' He said, 'Lord, I believe.' And he worshipped him. (Jn 9:11, 17, 33, 36-38)

FEATURE 5

'If you love me, keep my word'

If people open up to us, and especially if it is to reveal something intimate about themselves, the basic response they seek is that we listen to what they have to say. They also want us to respond in an honest way to what they reveal to us. This listening and responding is the key way we learn to believe in those who believe in us. It is also the key way we can bring about the change of mind and heart that is involved if we are to believe things about ourselves that are contrary to what we already believe. As friends listen to each other they gradually adjust to the ways they are chosen and trusted, accepted and affirmed by one another. By responding honestly to this acceptance and affirmation, they both intensify the positive feelings aroused by what they hear and they overcome their resistance to it.

The basic response Jesus calls for when he reveals himself to us is that we would be sensitive and responsive to his self-revelation, that we would 'hear the word of God and do it'. This is the condition of our entry into the intimate relationship he wants to establish with us.

> Then his mother and his brothers came to him, but they could not reach him because of the crowd. And he was told, 'Your mother and your brothers are standing outside, wanting to see you.' But he said to them, 'My mother and my brothers are those who hear the word of God and do it.' (Lk 8:19-21)

In the parable of the sower, Jesus paints a picture of the various ways people listen and respond to his word or self-revelation. The first three responses he depicts are inadequate so that the seed, which represents the word of God, does not bear any fruit. Those in whom the word does bear fruit listen to his revelation and respond by 'holding it fast in an honest and good heart'. (Lk 8:11-15)

In the parable of the Pharisee and the tax collector, Jesus asks us to face an important element of the friendship he wants to draw us into. This is that in our friendship with him we honestly face who we are and who he is. In the parable, Jesus commends the way the tax collector comes before God with an attitude of humility and reverence. Contrasted with this is the attitude of the Pharisee. He is self-righteous and lacks humility, respect and gratitude. He gives way to our human tendency to reduce our response to God's self-revelation to carrying out our 'spiritual duties' or to the formal observance of a body of rules and ritual. We thus tend to hide what is really in our hearts behind the respectable front of outward observance.

> Two men went up to the temple to pray, one a Pharisee and the other a tax collector. The Pharisee, standing by himself, was praying thus, 'God, I thank you that I am not like other people: thieves, rogues, adulterers, or even like this tax collector. I fast twice a week; I give a tenth of all my income.' But the tax collector, standing far off, would not even look up to heaven, but was beating his breast and saying, 'God, be merciful to me, a sinner!' I tell you, this man went down to his home justified rather than the other; for all who exalt themselves will be humbled, but all who humble themselves will be exalted.' (Lk 18:9-14)

It is above all in the Mass that Jesus provides us with the opportunity to enter fully the friendship he wishes to establish with us. It is in this dramatic presentation of the extent and depth of his love that Jesus invites us to savour and assimilate this love which is the basis of our friendship with him. (Jn 6:52-59) It is in the Mass too that we can most effectively express how we feel about his laying down his life for us his friends. (Jn 15:13-14) In doing this we 'abide in' his love just as he abides in his Father's love; we immerse our whole person, 'heart, soul, strength and mind', in receiving and returning his love in the way the commandments invite us to. (Lk 10:25-28)

> As the Father has loved me, so I have loved you; abide in my love. If you keep my commandments, you will abide in my love, just as I have kept my Father's commandments and abide in his love ... You are my friends if you do what I command you. (Jn 15:9-15)

FEATURE 6

Maintaining our friendship with Jesus

If we are to maintain our friendships we need to communicate with our friends on a regular basis; we must make the space to listen and respond to them. Listening involves taking the time to savour and to surrender to the unique truth that others share with us. We have then to respond honestly to what we hear, giving expression to both the positive and negative feelings aroused by what we have listened to. If we listen and respond in this way to what others reveal to us about themselves we cannot avoid developing an intimate relationship with them. We will experience the truth of the saying that 'a relationship is as good as the communication going on within it'. This kind of honest communication does not come easily to us. It is hard to make the space necessary to listen to our inmost self and to that of another. Responding honestly to what we have heard another say is also difficult as it requires that we become aware of our feelings and take the pains to reveal them.

It is through such a conversation that Jesus wishes to develop and maintain the friendship he initiates with us. In this conversation we listen to Jesus revealing himself to us and we respond to what we hear him say. By listening to him he puts us in touch with our essential goodness and this stirs up a lot of feeling which we need to share with him in an honest way. The foundation for this conversation was laid when Jesus became a human being and thus the focal point of revelation and of our response to it. To emphasise this fact Jesus draws on one of the richest symbols of the Old Covenant, that of the ladder in Jacob's dream stretching between heaven and earth. (Gen 28:10-22)

> Very truly, I tell you, you will see heaven opened and the angels of God ascending and descending upon the Son of Man. (Jn 1:52)

Like all the miracles of Jesus the healing of the deaf mute has a significance that is beyond the physical healing. In other words this miracle highlights Jesus' concern to open our ears so that we may listen to his word and to loosen our tongue so that we may respond honestly to the way he acknowledges, accepts and affirms us in his revelation.

> They brought to him a deaf man who had an impediment in his speech; and they begged him to lay his hand on him. He took him aside in private, away from the crowd, and put his fingers into his ears, and he spat and touched his tongue. Then looking up to heaven, he sighed and said to him, 'Ephphatha,' that is, 'Be opened.' And immediately his ears were opened, his tongue was released, and he spoke plainly. (Mk 7:32-35)

When we reflect on how we are empowered to listen and respond to Jesus we may find a new relevance in the scene in the gospel where Jesus commends Mary for listening to him. For an age that underrates a contemplative stance to life and overrates an active one, what Jesus says to Martha about her excessive activity is particularly pertinent.

> Martha, Martha, you are worried and distracted by many things; there is need of only one thing. Mary has chosen the better part, which will not be taken away from her. (Lk 10:41-42)

Jesus repeatedly emphasises our need for this contemplative stance to life, for real leisure and for what he terms 'rest'. This rest is required if we are to find the space or the time, the energy and the resources that we need to maintain the friendship Jesus wants to establish with us.

> Come away to a deserted place all by yourselves and rest a while. For many were coming and going, and they had no leisure even to eat. (Mk 6:31) Come to me, all you that are weary and are carrying heavy burdens, and I will give you rest. Take my yoke upon you, and learn from me; for I am gentle and humble in heart, and you will find rest for your souls. For my yoke is easy, and my burden is light.' (Mt 11:28-30)

FEATURE 7

'That you may be one just as we are one'

When friends take the trouble to establish and maintain a friendship, a strong bond forms between them. The closeness of this bond will depend not just on the quality of the sharing but on what they share. As we have seen, it is the love that underlies all we share that more than anything else creates this bond and sustains it. 'It is care that makes and sustains us.' This care we experience from our friends is a growing sense of being chosen by and of being entrusted with a part of themselves they do not share with others. There is also a growing sense of being accepted and appreciated that leads to a sense of being important for one another. All these forms of love that characterise friendship create and maintain a very strong bond that becomes such a major feature of friendship that Aristotle could say, 'Friendship is a single soul dwelling in two bodies.' *(Aristotle)*

In chapters 3-12 of the book of Genesis the story of the Fall is described as a gradual disintegration of society which occurred when it separated itself from God. Jesus comes to reintegrate us and all things so that we are reunited with him. The growth of the bond Jesus brings about in this way is a major theme in John's gospel, where he sees the work of Jesus as 'gathering into one the dispersed children of God'.

> Jesus was about to die for the nation, and not for the nation only, but to gather into one the dispersed children of God. (Jn 11:49-52)

It is the attractiveness of Jesus that is the magnetic force that gathers people around him so that even his enemies acknowledge the fact that 'the whole world is running after him'. 'The Pharisees then said to one another, 'You see, you can do nothing. Look, the whole world is running after him!' (Jn 12:19) The ultimate source of this integrating power of Jesus is the definitive sign he gives when he loves us 'to the end', or to the utmost extent.

> Now before the festival of the Passover, Jesus knew that his hour had come to depart from this world and go to the

Father. Having loved his own who were in the world, he loved them to the end. (Jn 13:1)

If we savour the glimpses the Spirit gives us of being loved 'to the end', it gives us an intimate knowledge of the profound reality that we are loved by Jesus just as he loves the Father and as the Father loves him. 'As the Father has loved me, so I have loved you; abide in my love. (Jn 15:9) ... (You) have loved them even as you have loved me.' (Jn 17:23) When we learn to abide in Jesus' love both he, the Father and the Spirit make their home in us.

> Those who love me will keep my word, and my Father will love them, and we will come to them and make our home with them. (Jn 14:23)

In sharing their love in this way they draw us into an environment that is as all-encompassing as the love that draws us into it. This environment in which Jesus wants to share 'everything' of his life with the Father and the Spirit, the union that the splendour of their love draws us into, is what Jesus calls *friendship*. 'I have called you friends, because I have made known to you everything that I have heard from my Father.' This friendship which Jesus seeks to establish with us is such a profound and permanent union that Jesus speaks of it as being complete; it is a share in the union that the three persons of the Trinity enjoy. 'That they may all be one. As you, Father, are in me and I am in you, may they also be in us, so that the world may believe that you have sent me. The glory that you have given me I have given them, so that they may be one, as we are one.' (17:21-22) In this union we experience what life is like within the Trinity as we say with and in Jesus, 'Abba! Father!'.

> For all who are led by the Spirit of God are children of God. For you have received a spirit of adoption. When we cry, 'Abba! Father!' it is that very Spirit bearing witness with our spirit that we are children of God, and if children, then heirs, heirs of God and joint heirs with Christ. (Rom 8:14-17)

It is through the Mass that Jesus seeks to build up and to maintain this friendship in which we live in him and he lives in us. (Jn 6:54-56)